Learning Bootstrap 4 Building Projects

Develop 5 real-world Bootstrap 4.x projects from scratch

Eduonix Learning Solutions

BIRMINGHAM - MUMBAI

Learning Bootstrap 4 by Building Projects

Commissioning Editor: Amarabha Banerjee
Acquisition Editor: Shweta Pant
Content Development Editor: Arun Nadar
Technical Editor: Leena Patil
Copy Editor: Safis Editing
Project Coordinator: Sheejal Shah
Proofreader: Safis Editing
Indexer: Rekha Nair
Graphics: Jason Monteiro
Production Coordinator: Shantanu Zagade

First published: August 2018

Production reference: 1310818

Published by Packt Publishing Ltd.
Livery Place
35 Livery Street
Birmingham
B3 2PB, UK.

ISBN 978-1-78934-325-0

www.packtpub.com

mapt.io

Mapt is an online digital library that gives you full access to over 5,000 books and videos, as well as industry leading tools to help you plan your personal development and advance your career. For more information, please visit our website.

Why subscribe?

- Spend less time learning and more time coding with practical eBooks and Videos from over 4,000 industry professionals

- Improve your learning with Skill Plans built especially for you

- Get a free eBook or video every month

- Mapt is fully searchable

- Copy and paste, print, and bookmark content

PacktPub.com

Did you know that Packt offers eBook versions of every book published, with PDF and ePub files available? You can upgrade to the eBook version at www.PacktPub.com and as a print book customer, you are entitled to a discount on the eBook copy. Get in touch with us at service@packtpub.com for more details.

At www.PacktPub.com, you can also read a collection of free technical articles, sign up for a range of free newsletters, and receive exclusive discounts and offers on Packt books and eBooks.

Contributors

About the author

Eduonix Learning Solutions creates and distributes high quality technology training content. Our team of industry professionals have been training manpower for more than a decade.

We aim to teach technology the way it is used in industry and professional world. We have professional team of trainers for technologies ranging from Mobility, Web to Enterprise and Database and Server Administration.

Packt is searching for authors like you

If you're interested in becoming an author for Packt, please visit authors.packtpub.com and apply today. We have worked with thousands of developers and tech professionals, just like you, to help them share their insight with the global tech community. You can make a general application, apply for a specific hot topic that we are recruiting an author for, or submit your own idea.

Table of Contents

Preface

We have come a long way from the first websites that were dull and full of text. While they served their purpose back then, today, websites need to be more dynamic and interactive. In addition to fulfilling their purpose, they must also look aesthetically appeasing.

Websites are primarily designed in HTML and CSS, with HTML being used for the structure and CSS helping with the design and the look-and-feel of the website. Having to code every inch of a website can often be a tedious task, which is why there are templates or frameworks that can be modified to get the desired layout of the website.

Bootstrap is this, and so much more! Bootstrap is a framework that provides a template or a layout that can be used as is or can be modified. It allows you to add items such as jumbotrons, lightboxes, sticky menus, and so much more without have to write the tedious coding that's behind it.

Bootstrap 4, the latest version, is a complete rewrite of the older versions. It offers more support and makes it easier to integrate the framework into your website design. It now comes with features such as switching from LESS to Sass, added support for Flexbox, and dropped support for IE8, IE9, and iOS 6. It has also increased the global font size to 16 px, switched from pixels to root ems, and have even rewritten all the components and jQuery plugins.

This version of Bootstrap requires learning things from scratch, and this is exactly what we are offering. We have designed this book to simplify getting your hands on Bootstrap and actually learn using an example-based approach.

In this book, you will get down to the nitty-gritty of Bootstrap 4 by actually building projects in Bootstrap from the ground up. Using five projects, you will learn the different components and features, all the while learning exactly how to put it into use.

The book has been designed in a manner that will help breakdown Bootstrap for you, and won't talk over your head. So, if you have zero experience with Bootstrap, this book has got your covered.

Who this book is for

If you are a web developer who wants to build real-world responsive website from scratch using Bootstrap 4, then this book is for you. Basic knowledge of HTML and CSS is required.

What this book covers

Chapter 1, *Introduction*, starts the book off with an introduction to Bootstrap.

Chapter 2, *Bootstrap 4 Features*, introduces you to all the new features that Bootstrap 4 offers. You will learn how to set up the environment before you start building your projects.

Chapter 3, *Photosharing Website*, helps you create multiple pages with different layouts. You will be introduced to Font Awesome and media breakpoints.

Chapter 4, *Building a Resume Website*, teaches you how to create a sophisticated resume site where you will be using the Bootstrap grid system to create layouts for your different sections, such as about me, contact information, education, experience, skills, services, and recent projects.

Chapter 5, *Social Network Frontend*, covers a number of different features, such as creating bubble comments, adding photos, and creating groups. You will also learn how to add a sidebar to the website.

Chapter 6, *Agency Website*, helps you build a one-page Bootstrap website where you will have a navigation menu and a jumbotron. You will also learn some JavaScript animation to achieve a smooth scrolling effect.

Chapter 7, *Lightbox Website*, uses the lightbox plugin to create a gallery of photos with two different layout. You will also learn how to create a carousel, which is basically a image slideshow.

To get the most out of this book

For this book, you will need Visual Studio Code to write our HTML, CSS, and JavaScript codes. You can use any browser (Chrome, Safari, or Firefox) to see the results of the website that you are building. Basic knowledge of HTML and CSS is required.

Download the example code files

You can download the example code files for this book from your account at www.packtpub.com. If you purchased this book elsewhere, you can visit www.packtpub.com/support and register to have the files emailed directly to you.

You can download the code files by following these steps:

1. Log in or register at www.packtpub.com.
2. Select the **SUPPORT** tab.
3. Click on **Code Downloads & Errata**.
4. Enter the name of the book in the **Search** box and follow the onscreen instructions.

Once the file is downloaded, please make sure that you unzip or extract the folder using the latest version of:

- WinRAR/7-Zip for Windows
- Zipeg/iZip/UnRarX for Mac
- 7-Zip/PeaZip for Linux

The code bundle for the book is also hosted on GitHub at https://github.com/PacktPublishing/Learning-Bootstrap-4-by-Building-Projects. In case there's an update to the code, it will be updated on the existing GitHub repository.

We also have other code bundles from our rich catalog of books and videos available at https://github.com/PacktPublishing/. Check them out!

Download the color images

We also provide a PDF file that has color images of the screenshots/diagrams used in this book. You can download it here: https://www.packtpub.com/sites/default/files/downloads/LearningBootstrap4byBuildingProjects_ColorImages.pdf.

Conventions used

There are a number of text conventions used throughout this book.

CodeInText: Indicates code words in text, database table names, folder names, filenames, file extensions, pathnames, dummy URLs, user input, and Twitter handles. Here is an example: "What they're doing here is creating a variable called $font-stack and assigning it the values Helvetica and sans-serif."

A block of code is set as follows:

```
$font-stack: Helvetica, sans-serif;
$primary-color: #333;

body {
 font: 100% $font-stack;
 color: $primary-color;
}
```

Any command-line input or output is written as follows:

```
npm install jquery
```

Bold: Indicates a new term, an important word, or words that you see onscreen. For example, words in menus or dialog boxes appear in the text like this. Here is an example: "We will go ahead and open the terminal, and now, let's go to the **Menu**, then **View**, and click on **Integrated Terminal**."

Warnings or important notes appear like this.

Tips and tricks appear like this.

Get in touch

Feedback from our readers is always welcome.

General feedback: Email feedback@packtpub.com and mention the book title in the subject of your message. If you have questions about any aspect of this book, please email us at questions@packtpub.com.

Errata: Although we have taken every care to ensure the accuracy of our content, mistakes do happen. If you have found a mistake in this book, we would be grateful if you would report this to us. Please visit www.packtpub.com/submit-errata, selecting your book, clicking on the Errata Submission Form link, and entering the details.

Piracy: If you come across any illegal copies of our works in any form on the Internet, we would be grateful if you would provide us with the location address or website name. Please contact us at copyright@packtpub.com with a link to the material.

If you are interested in becoming an author: If there is a topic that you have expertise in and you are interested in either writing or contributing to a book, please visit authors.packtpub.com.

Reviews

Please leave a review. Once you have read and used this book, why not leave a review on the site that you purchased it from? Potential readers can then see and use your unbiased opinion to make purchase decisions, we at Packt can understand what you think about our products, and our authors can see your feedback on their book. Thank you!

For more information about Packt, please visit packtpub.com.

Introduction 1

This book is a practical guide that will help you create modern-day apps with the use of Bootstrap 4, a powerful JavaScript library. It starts off with an introduction to Bootstrap, where we learn about some of the differences coming into Bootstrap 4 that didn't exist in Bootstrap 3. We will also be covering the new features that Bootstrap 4 offers. So, let's start with the sites that we have: we've got a photo-sharing site; this is going to use a lightbox and it's also our first introduction to using Bootstrap 4. Now, Bootstrap has a strict grid column setup where you have 12 columns, but you can divide them up in any way you like. We're also going to look at how you can even go outside the 12, which is a limit for Bootstrap. For example, you have added two columns of span 5 and 10 respectively; basically, when you sum up they're going out of the 12, but things still kind of work out mostly in the same way. So, depending on the complexity of your website, you miss and you go over the 12, we're still going to see things work out pretty much fine.

Next, we have our resume site, which gets a little more complex because of the layout. We're going to use multiple rows, and we're going to have our columns deal with the different kinds of icons. Later on, we will check out **Font Awesome**, which is really going to come into play when we start getting into some of the more complex websites, because we're not actually using icon images, we're using Font Awesome instead, which acts as a font but really gives us icons. We'll look at a social networking website, where we're going to learn what cards are all about. We're going to look at how to create bubble-style comments, and some other different kinds of more complex layout features to get a particular kind of look to your page. Next is the agency website—a very clean, very nice-looking website. It's going to make heavy use of Font Awesome and some of the different icons that are available to us. Then we'll look at another photo site that we're going to integrate with a different lightbox that doesn't require JavaScript.

There is a lot going on. We're going to go through a great introduction and get some hands-on practice with Bootstrap 4, so let's jump into it.

2
Bootstrap 4 Features

In this chapter, we are going to learn about Bootstrap 4. We will basically get a general introduction to how Bootstrap works through the Hello-World program that we're going to create. This chapter starts off by introducing you to the changes that Bootstrap 4 offers. These changes are pretty exciting, and there are some good changes regarding the grids, fonts, and a lot of other things. We will go into detail about what these new changes are. We will then look into the code editor that we're going to use – it's free, popular, easy to use, and it's cross-platform as well.

We will then get into initializing a new Bootstrap 4 project. Different people have their own ways of doing this — you can either work with the **Content Delivery Network (CDN)**, which means you're always going to be dependent on an internet connection, or you can bring it in locally. These are the two main ways to initialize a Bootstrap project. We will look at both of these ways, but we will focus on bringing it locally so that we can have everything contained in our local environment and not have to depend on the internet, because this allows you then to work without an internet connection. There's a specific way we're going to set it up — just in the same way regarding how folders are laid out inside of a project — and we're also going to use a tool to help us with our **Syntactically awesome style sheets (Sass)**, pre-processing, and the running of different tasks. This means that we're going to have a task runner, and we're going to see how that's going to help us move files around and keep things organized as well.

We will then give you a quick introduction to Sass. If you are not familiar with Sass, this chapter will help you understand what it is and why we're wanting to use it inside of Bootstrap 4. In fact, Bootstrap has moved from **Leaner Style Sheets** (**LESS**) to Sass, so if you're familiar with LESS, that's kind of gone away, and we're going to see how our task runner is going to help us with the precompilation of Sass.

So, speaking of task runners, we have Gulp. Gulp is going to do a few things for us; it's going to do the precompilation from Sass to CSS, so we're no longer writing in CSS files – we're just writing in Sass files. Even if you want to write just straight CSS, you could do so, but you need to do it in a Sass file because the CSS file will get overwritten when we run the Gulp task. Therefore, Gulp is going to move JavaScript files from the Bootstrap distribution folder into our project, it's going to move CSS files, it's going to do the compilation for Sass, and it's also going to launch our web browser. It's going to run all of these tasks when we type in Gulp and then it's going to launch our web browser for us. This is going to be part of our workflow and it's going to be fairly streamlined.

Once we have all of that going on and we have our project layout done, we're going to create a simple Hello-World program and see how that works now that everything is in place.

After we have the project folder structures laid out, the files are placed, and we have Gulp fully integrated, we're going to see how everything works from that point on. This is going to be our template as we create and move into these different projects that we're going to be building.

What's new in Bootstrap 4 – introducing new features

In this section, we're going to see what's new in Bootstrap 4. As we go through this book, we're also going to see examples of these new features in action as we build up our different projects.

Bootstrap 4 has got quite a few new features and we will be looking at the more popular ones. **Flexbox** is one of the main features that has been added, also known as **CSS3 Flexible Box**, and it's used a lot with the grid. It allows you to accomplish the more popular layouts as well as complex layouts easily, so if you were trying to do the same thing in CSS, it would be a little more difficult and challenging. Therefore, we're going to see how Flexbox really helps make the different kinds of layout that you want to achieve in an easier manner.

LESS has been replaced with Sass, so we will see a few examples of Sass and how to make use of it, how to compile it, and get it into our CSS.

Some of the JavaScript has been rewritten in ES6 so that it has the latest standards and a lot of compatibility and good performance as well, and this relates to some of their plugins that have JavaScript. Other, different areas, of JavaScript have also been updated.

It also added cards and Font Awesome, so we're going to take a look at cards in a little bit and learn about how those are used. Then, we have **Glyphs**, which are replaced with Font Awesome.

There's a new grid tier for smaller devices that are 576px and below. Here, some of the grid columns and the different ways of accessing the grid layout have been changed. So, when we go and check the website, we will see all of these changes mentioned there.

Next, we have Tether, which is a JavaScript utility that's used for UI placement and tooltips, so we'll see how Tether integrates. It's actually a call at the bottom of your main page if you check out the `index.html` file, which is where we had the three references for JavaScript: one for jQuery, one for Tether, and one for the Bootstrap JavaScript reference, which needs to go last since it depends on the other two.

Migrating to v4

Without further ado, open your favorite browser and visit the *Migrating to Bootstrap 4* documentation page at `https://getbootstrap.com/docs/4.0/migration/`:

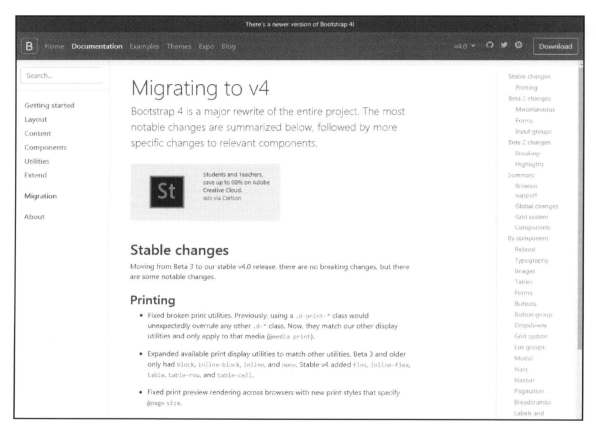

As you can see on the **Migrating to v4** documentation page, there are several things on the left, and at the bottom we have **Migration**. Here, you will see a lot of the different changes that Bootstrap 4 introduced, of which a few were discussed earlier. It has dropped the support for IE8, IE9, and iOS6, which is only for IE10+ and iOS 7+. It has mobile browser support as well.

In the **Global changes** section, you will see some of the big changes. Flexbox is enabled by default, so they're getting away from things such as floats; they've switched from LESS to Sass for CSS; and another thing is they're favoring rems instead of px. px is still being used, but there's a lot more move toward rem, and the global font size has been increased from 14 to 16, which is interesting. This probably has a lot to do with accessibility, since you get more screens with retina, and they also revamped grid tiers to address the smaller devices which are 576px or below, as mentioned earlier.

You will also see that major updates have been done to the grid system, such as the use of Flexbox and the use of the new attribute naming.

Then, we have components where they've dropped the **Glyphicons** and instead added Font Awesome. It also has octicons, cards, and so on.

Under **Utilities**, you will find **Flex**. The following screenshot shows an example of what this looks like. It has simple to really complex alignments, it's pretty involved, and as you shrink the browser, everything stays as it is:

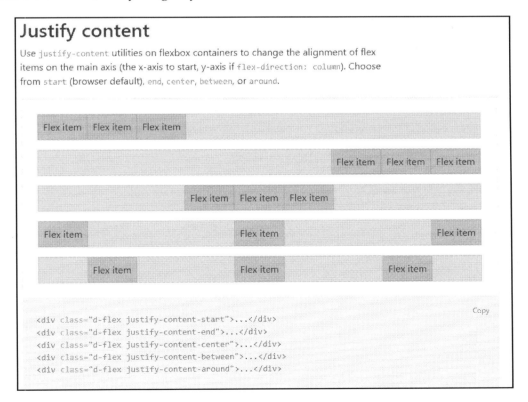

We have a few more types of layouts, such as the following one, where you can individually change their alignments:

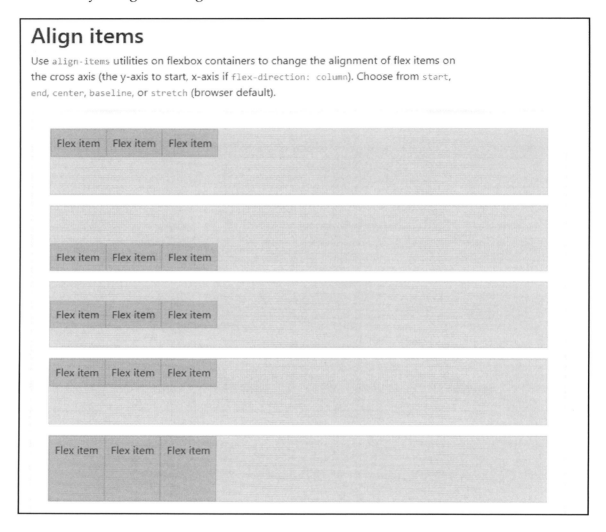

Now, let's look at cards, which come under **Components**. We will look at a few examples of cards and what they look like. The following screenshot shows an example of the **Card** where you can put an image up at the top, and then you can introduce some content and also include a button, like so:

```
<div class="card" style="width: 18rem;">
  <img class="card-img-top" src="..." alt="Card image cap">
  <div class="card-body">
    <h5 class="card-title">Card title</h5>
    <p class="card-text">Some quick example text to build on the card title and make up the bul
    <a href="#" class="btn btn-primary">Go somewhere</a>
  </div>
</div>
```

We will use a card that will look like the previous one, which introduces three horizontally aligned boxes. This just gives it a really good layout. You can see that they've got round corners (you can go square if you want), so there's a lot of different things you can do there regarding customization.

Here is one more example where we just have the text. You can add links, but it won't have a button:

Titles, text, and links

Card titles are used by adding .card-title to a <h*> tag. In the same way, links are added and placed next to each other by adding .card-link to an <a> tag.

Subtitles are used by adding a .card-subtitle to a <h*> tag. If the .card-title and the .card-subtitle items are placed in a .card-body item, the card title and subtitle are aligned nicely.

Card title
Card subtitle

Some quick example text to build on the card title and make up the bulk of the card's content.

Card link   Another link

Copy

```
<div class="card" style="width: 18rem;">
  <div class="card-body">
    <h5 class="card-title">Card title</h5>
    <h6 class="card-subtitle mb-2 text-muted">Card subtitle</h6>
    <p class="card-text">Some quick example text to build on the card title and make up the bul
    <a href="#" class="card-link">Card link</a>
    <a href="#" class="card-link">Another link</a>
  </div>
</div>
```

We also have a big card with all the different components in it:

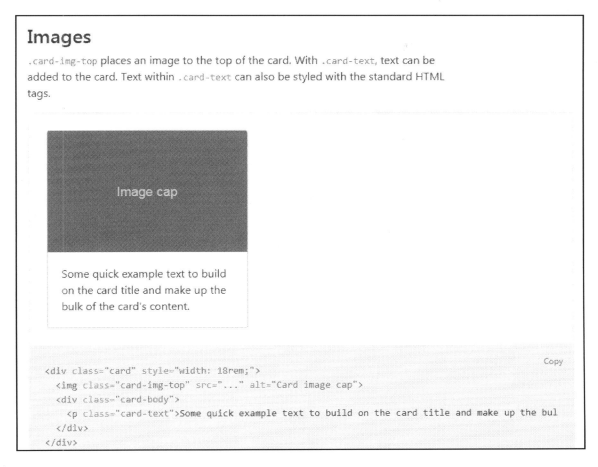

So, that's what cards are. Now, let's check out Reboot. It is similar to normalized, which we had in the previous version of Bootstrap. It is another way of correcting inconsistencies across browsers. When you're starting a whole new section in your web page, you used to have to perform normalize or clears to have the CSS above you not affect what you're doing, so Reboot has kind of taken that place.

Now, let's look at tether. On the documentation page, let's go to the **Tooltips** section under **Components**. Here, you can see that it is making use of tether for it to function. In the following screenshot, you can see how you can just place them in different areas and align them however you want. The default is on the top, such as the one shown in the following screenshot, so if you have some text, or a paragraph of text, you can just highlight a word in there and the tooltip will appear above it:

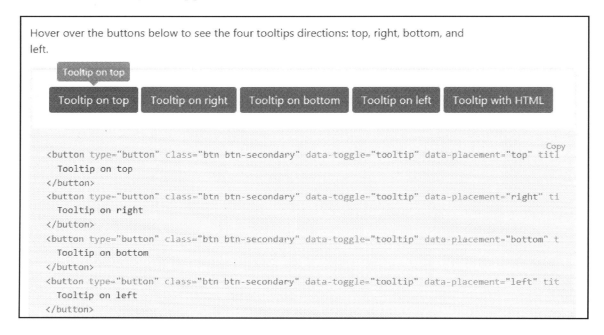

There's a lot of customization as to how you want it to look, so that is where you get a lot of use out of tether. These are pretty much all the features that we are going to use as we walk through our different projects.

Setting up the code editor

We are going to use the **Visual Studio Code (VS Code)** editor for our book. Let's go to `https://code.visualstudio.com/`, where you can go to the home page and learn more about the editor. Of course, as we go through this book, we're going to learn about what we need to know rather than just go through everything and do a whole tour of this editor, but here are some basics about the editor.

It's cross-platform, so you can use it on Windows or Mac, and it's free to use. One of the reasons I really prefer using this editor is, other than it being a great editor, you have an integrated terminal so you don't have to keep going out to your terminal or command line to run different commands on the command prompt. So, you can stay right here, inside of your editor, and pretty much do everything. As we move forward through this book, the two important tools that we are going to use are the editor and the web browser, and that really makes things fairly simple with regard to our development environment and the kind of workflows that we're going to be using. So, to get VS Code on your machine, go ahead and download it. I'm on a Mac, so, as you can see here, click **Download for Mac**. You also have the other different operating systems that you can download it for, but it should just auto-detect whatever you're on, so go ahead and install it:

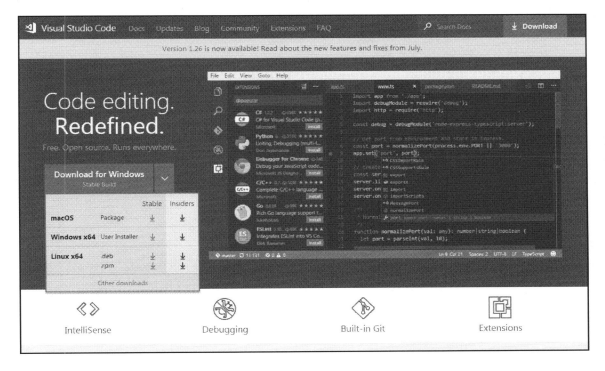

While you're installing it, one thing to keep an eye out for — which should happen at the beginning of the installation — is questions asking whether you want to integrate depending on your OS, whether you want to integrate with finder, or whether you want to integrate with Windows Explorer, or add a shortcut so that you can quickly launch VS Code. In your terminal, you can just type in the code and it will launch VS Code from the folder that you're in, which makes things really easy because it will open and have that folder there. You can go ahead and add your files, and do any kind of folder exploration that you need to do right there inside of VS Code. So, let's open the command prompt and launch VS Code, and you'll see the shortcut that we talked about. We will also get to see the IDE in action.

Here is the command prompt, as well as a folder I've created for this project called `hello-world`:

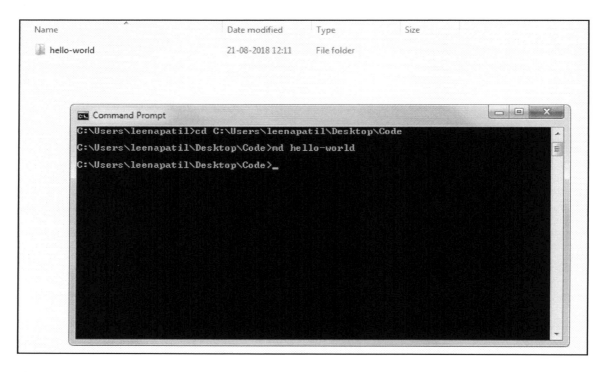

If we go ahead and check the contents by typing `ls`, for Windows users you can check by `dir`, you will see that there's nothing in this folder at all. Now, let's launch VS Code right from this folder using a shortcut method. Here, we will type `code` . as shown in the following screenshot:

`hello-world` on the left pane, as shown in the following screenshot:

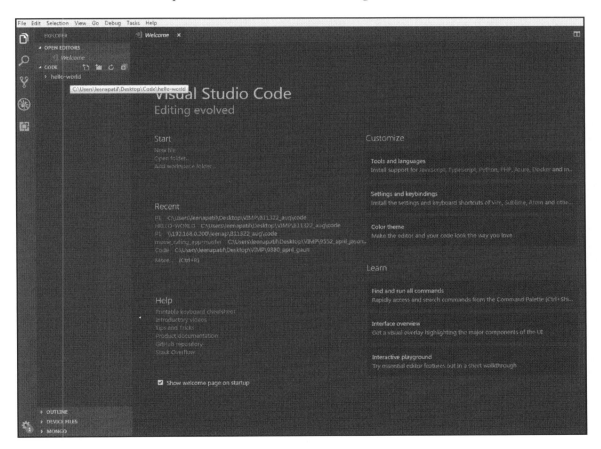

We will go ahead and open the terminal, and now, let's go to the **Menu**, then **View**, and click on **Integrated Terminal**. Below this, our command prompt will appear inside that folder, and if we use `ls` or `dir`, you will see that, once again, there's nothing there. This is really convenient so that we don't have to worry about going out to our terminal:

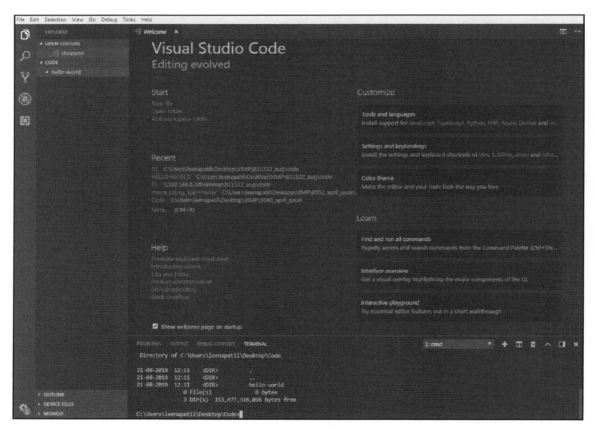

As you can see from the preceding screenshot, this is what VS Code looks like. On the left is where our folders and our files are going to appear, so this is our subfolders in this case. I'm going to create a file just by clicking on the plus sign and clicking **New File**. We will call it index.html, and in the following screenshot, you can see that it is open:

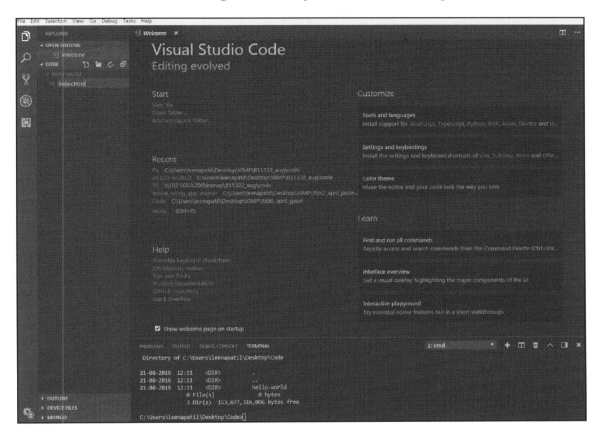

So, here's our Welcome page. Let's close it by clicking the **x**, and open index.html, where we're going to paste in our code from Bootstrap. Then, we're going to check out what our first initial page looks like.

As you can see in the following screenshot, there are two plus signs besides the `hello-world` name. The first is for creating a new file, while the other one is for creating a new folder. We will create a new folder and call it `src`, and we will put `index.html` inside of `src`, as shown in the following screenshot:

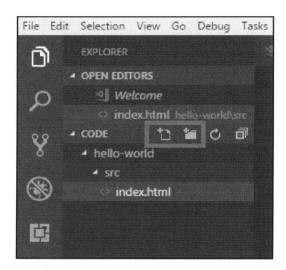

These are pretty much the basics. As we walk through this book, we will see code highlighting and the other features the editor has. If you're using something like Atom or some other popular text editors, they're going to work as normally as you would want them to. The way we're going to do this is through VS Code. You may have to jump out to the terminal, but if you're used to that workflow, it's probably not much of a big difference. So, next, what we're going to do is go ahead and get Bootstrap 4, initialize our project, and start moving forward with creating a simple Hello-World example so that we can see how everything comes together.

Initializing a new project

Let's go to the Bootstrap website at `https://getbootstrap.com`. If you want to get the current release, you can just click the **Download** button and do an installation. However, that's not the route we're going to take. Here, I'll show you how we're going to install Bootstrap:

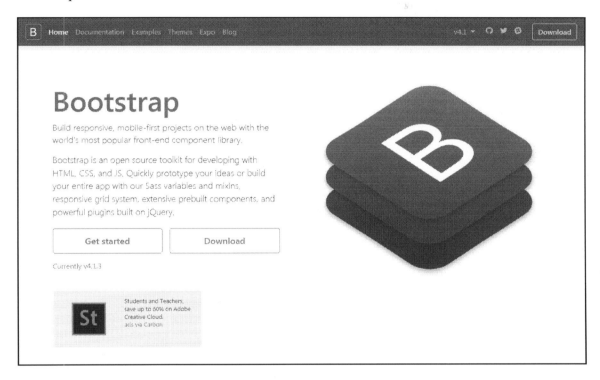

So, the current version is v4.1.3, as shown in the preceding screenshot. If you've never seen this website before, there's a lot of great documentation on Bootstrap. If you go to the menu and click on **Documentation**, we're going to use the **Quick start** to get the code going inside of VS Code. Then, we're going to do some initialization with another tool:

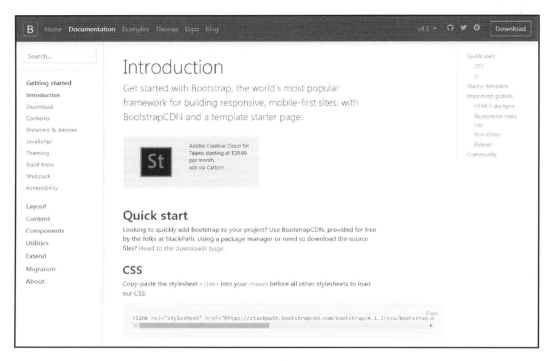

The website also has a few examples regarding what you can do with Bootstrap. You can check out these examples by clicking the **Examples** tab in the menu, as shown in the following screenshot:

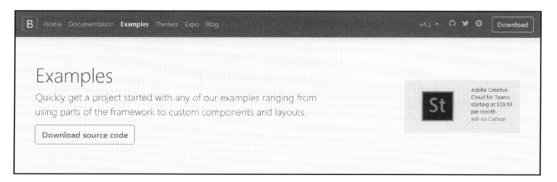

We're going to use a tool called npm, which is a package manager. So, if you haven't worked with package managers, the way they work is that you mainly use them through the command line, and some of them will integrate with your IDE. You can use the UI to download different packages. So, these packages are going to be things such as Bootstrap, jQuery, and Tether. We're going to use this tool to help us with builds, precompiling, and different kinds of tasks such as moving files called Gulp. This is all going to come from the package manager. So, to get the package manager, we will open a new tab in the browser and go to nodejs.org:

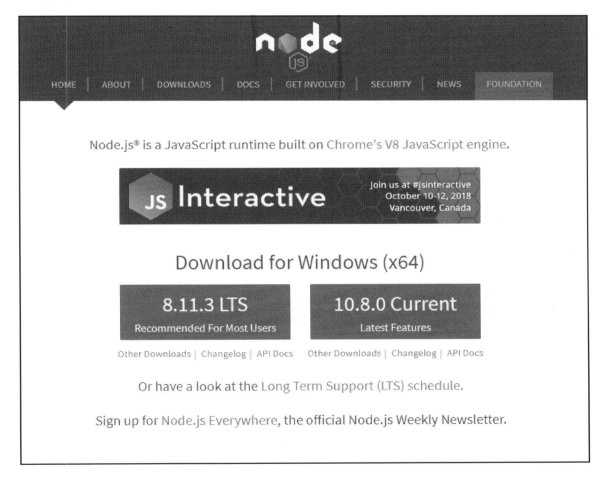

All you need to do here is download Node, which is going to have npm. It's going to give you everything you need on the backend to have the development environment running the way that we're going to want it to run. We're going to see how to use npm shortly.

But before that, what we are going to do is go back to the **Home** page of the Bootstrap website and scroll down, where we're going to see a few different ways to get Bootstrap onto our machines:

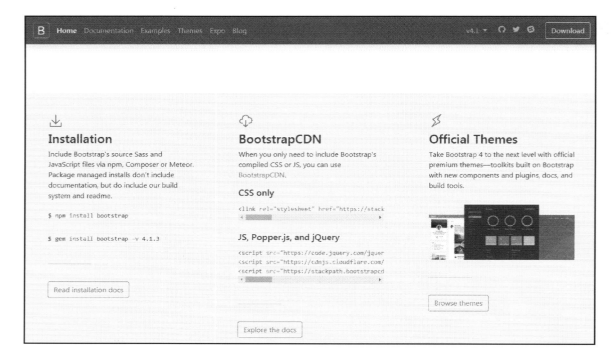

The quickest way to get Bootstrap, which we're going to look at first, is to use the CDN. We're actually going to get a starter template. Go to **Documentation** again, and over there on the right we will have the **Starter template**:

From here, we will copy all of the code shown in the Starter template and go back into VS Code, paste it in our index.html file, and hit save.

So, at this point, there's not much going on with the code we pasted, and we could go ahead and look at the result on the browser. This would be fairly simple to do, and in fact, we're going to go ahead and do just that. So, if we `ls` (or `dir`) now, you will see that we've got our `src` folder. If we go ahead and change directories, we can see that we've got our index.html file. So, again, everything we need is right here, inside this integrated terminal, as shown in the following screenshot:

Let's go ahead and open this into the browser:

Hello, world!

Alright, so there's our **Hello, world!** – very simple, but we are making a little bit of use of the fonts here. If we go ahead, right-click and **Inspect** this page, we will see everything that we need for Bootstrap. The CDN is present.

Now let's edit the attribute by right-clicking so that we have an invalid path. If you change the href under the Bootstrap <link> tag, you will see the difference between the previous screenshot and the following one. So, we're definitely making use of the Bootstrap file here from this CDN:

Now we're going to go back into VS Code, and we're going to start using the package managers. The first thing we're going to do is initialize our folder and go back out to the root. Let's type ls (dir for windows) in the terminal. We will see our src folder, and then we will type the following command:

```
npm init
```

So, after you've installed Node.js, you should be able to access npm from the command line, as shown in the following screenshot, and we will go ahead and hit *Enter*. There's going to be a few prompts here, and you can use a -y command-line switch if you just want to blow through all of these as I'm going to do here by pressing *Enter*. So, I'm just going to take the defaults of everything. Notice some of the values here. We have hello-world for the package name, the version, and we have our entry point file, called main:

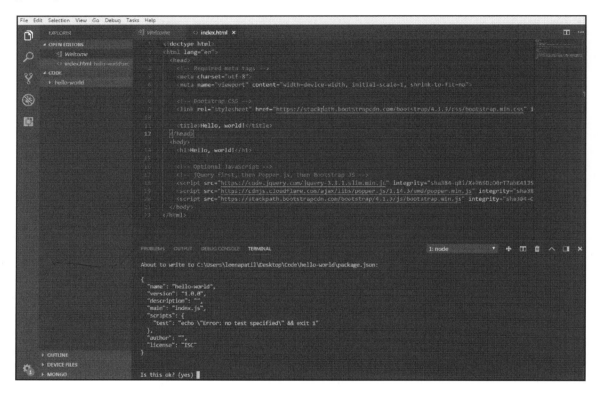

It's going to create a new file, `package.json`, just for npm's purposes, tell us what all the various dependencies are, and give it some metadata about our project:

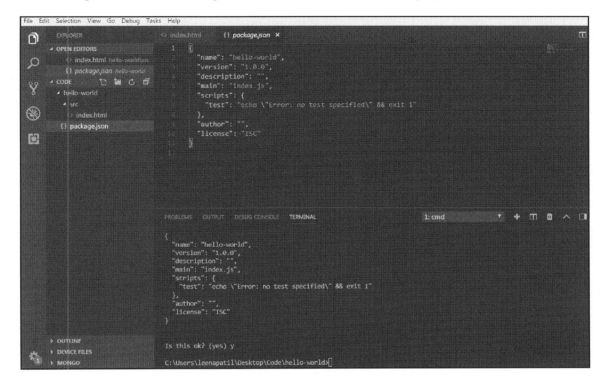

So, now we're going to install Bootstrap using the package manager. As we saw earlier, in the **Home** page of Bootstrap's website, we have a command for installing Bootstrap. We will copy the npm command, install Bootstrap, and paste this in VS Code's terminal and install it:

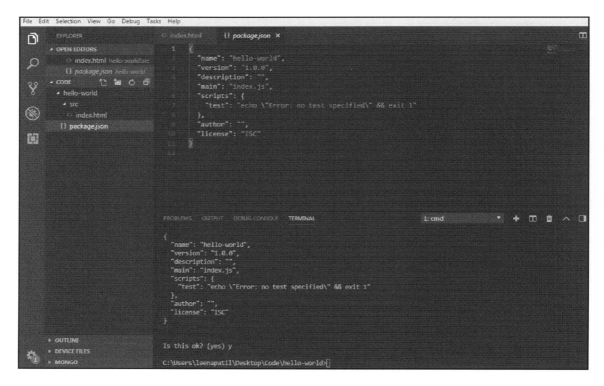

So, that's going to take just a little bit of time to download. Now we will get a new folder called node_modules. If we open node_modules, you will see that bootstrap is there, so all of our packages that we downloaded through npm are going to appear here, along with any of their dependencies:

```
Is this ok? (yes) y

C:\Users\leenapatil\Desktop\Code\hello-world>npm install bootstrap
npm WARN bootstrap@4.1.3 requires a peer of jquery@1.9.1 - 3 but none was installed.
npm WARN bootstrap@4.1.3 requires a peer of popper.js@^1.14.3 but none was installed.
npm WARN hello-world@1.0.0 No description
npm WARN hello-world@1.0.0 No repository field.

+ bootstrap@4.1.3
added 1 package in 4.266s

C:\Users\leenapatil\Desktop\Code\hello-world>
```

So, there are a few more packages that we're going to install. Here, we're going to do use the following:
For jQuery:

```
npm install jquery
```

It will show following on the terminal:

```
C:\Users\leenapatil\Desktop\Code\hello-world> npm install jquery
npm WARN hello-world@1.0.0 No description
npm WARN hello-world@1.0.0 No repository field.

+ jquery@3.3.1
added 45 packages, removed 163 packages and updated 238 packages in 54.296s
```

Then, we're going to get an npm install tether as well. Tether is used by Bootstrap 4 for UI layouts. You'll notice that it's not showing them under node_modules, which is because we haven't refreshed it yet, but those package folders are going to be inside of node_modules. For tether type following command:

```
npm install tether
```

It will show following on the terminal:

```
C:\Users\leenapatil\Desktop\Code\hello-world>npm install tether
npm WARN hello-world@1.0.0 No description
npm WARN hello-world@1.0.0 No repository field.

+ tether@1.4.4
added 1 package and removed 122 packages in 3.291s
```

In fact, if we change the directory to node_modules in the terminal and type ls (or dir), we can see that we have bootstrap, jquery, and tether.

Let's go back into the root. One thing we're going to also need is Gulp. Gulp is going to be used to compile our Sass into CSS, which we're going to explore a little bit more later. If you're new to Sass, you'll just get a very quick introduction to it, but you're going to see it being used quite a bit inside this book. Here, we will type the following command on the terminal:

```
npm install gulp browser-sync gulp-sass --save-dev
```

There are a few switches we need here. We're going to use browser-sync as well, which is actually going to do some injection for us into the browser. There's also gulp-sass, which is going to perform the precompilation of Sass into CSS.

This command is going to create a local dependency for this project rather than some kind of global installation:

```
C:\Users\leenapatil\Desktop\Code\hello-world>npm install gulp browser-sync gulp-sass --save-dev
npm WARN deprecated gulp-util@3.0.8: gulp-util is deprecated - replace it, following the guidelines at https://medium.com/gulpjs/
gulp-util-ca3b1f9f9ac5
npm WARN deprecated graceful-fs@3.0.11: please upgrade to graceful-fs 4 for compatibility with current and future versions of Nod
e.js
npm WARN deprecated minimatch@2.0.10: Please update to minimatch 3.0.2 or higher to avoid a RegExp DoS issue
npm WARN deprecated minimatch@0.2.14: Please update to minimatch 3.0.2 or higher to avoid a RegExp DoS issue
npm WARN deprecated graceful-fs@1.2.3: please upgrade to graceful-fs 4 for compatibility with current and future versions of Node
.js
npm WARN hello-world@1.0.0 No description
npm WARN hello-world@1.0.0 No repository field.
```

Upon hitting *Enter*, we're going to see some new dependencies pop up inside package.json once everything is completed and downloaded. Now we're going to make everything local. Right now, we have these CDNs that we are calling out to. We have to be connected to the internet to make use of these. We want our environment contained so that everything is local. That way, even if you're on an airplane and have no Wi-Fi, you can still work. A lot of this is going to come out of the node_modules folder. If you click on the refresh button and open the node_modules folder now, you will see that there's quite a few of them that have been added in there, as shown in the following screenshot:

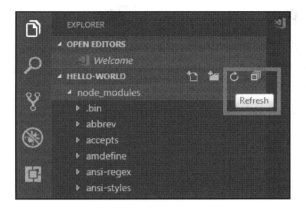

Now, we're going to change these routes, as shown in the following screenshot, so that we are using the local versions:

```
<link rel="stylesheet"
href="https://stackpath.bootstrapcdn.com/bootstrap/4.1.3/css/bootstrap.min.
css" integrity="sha384-
MCw98/SFnGE8fJT3GXwEOngsV7Zt27NXFoaoApmYm81iuXoPkFOJwJ8ERdknLPMO"
crossorigin="anonymous">
```

Here, we are going to change the location, which is pointing to our Bootstrap. So, what we want to do is create a folder that's going to contain our CSS, JavaScript, and Sass files. So, I'm going to close this node_modules. Inside src, we're going to create a js folder and a css folder, and we're going to have one more, which is for our scss files:

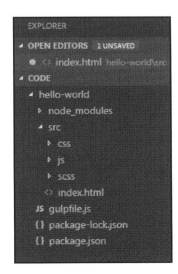

Then, we're going to change location under Bootstrap CSS code so that it's pointing to css, as shown in the following screenshot. Right now, we don't have a file under the `css` folder – we're going to take care of that a little bit later when we get into the use of Gulp. Let's go ahead and remove the metadata. We're going to have a `style.css` as well, and we're going to create that file/reference, as shown in the follows:

```
<!-- Bootstrap CSS -->
<link rel="stylesheet" href="/css/bootstrap.min.css" >
<link rel="stylesheet" href="/css/style.css" >
```

Now, under the Optional JavaScript code, we're going to put in a reference to `js/jquery.min.js` by removing some of the metadata. So, the next JS we're going to have is a tether. We're going to do one more, which is going to be a Bootstrap. Bootstrap is the last one in this chain because it's going to be dependent on these other two, as shown in the follows:

```
<!-- jQuery first, then Popper.js, then Bootstrap JS -->
<script src="/js/jquery.min.js" ></script>
<script src="/js/tether.min.js" ></script>
<script src="/js/bootstrapc.min.js" ></script>
```

Alright, so now the basic layout of this HTML file looks a little bit different, at least as far as the code goes. We're no longer dependent on these external files that we have to retrieve from the internet, so now we can work locally. Of course, we need to get these files into their proper locations, and that's what we're going to do next.

A quick introduction to Sass

In this section, we're going to look at a quick introduction to Sass, so for anyone who's never used Sass, this is just going to get you up to speed on what it is and why we want to use it. If you have used it, this is just going to be a quick refresher. So, let's go to sass-lang.com:

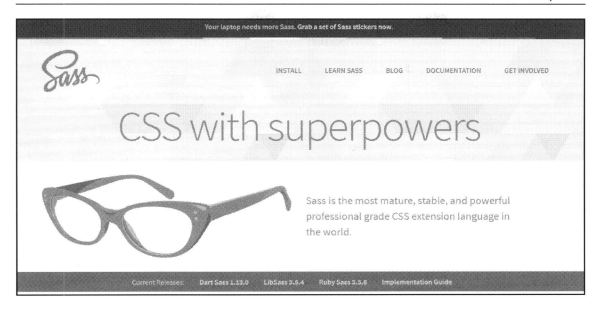

This is the website where you can learn all about Sass, and the documentation is also really good. If you want to explore more than what we're going to do here, this is the place to go to. So, if we go into **LEARN SASS**, you can really get a quick introduction into how it's used.

If you scroll down the page, you will see an SCSS syntax, as shown in the following code. We're going to basically make use of variables periodically. If you've ever used Ruby, this might look familiar, since it's written in Ruby:

```
$font-stack: Helvetica, sans-serif;
$primary-color: #333;

body {
  font: 100% $font-stack;
  color: $primary-color;
}
```

What they're doing here is creating a variable called $font-stack and assigning it the values Helvetica and sans-serif. The following code looks like CSS, where we have font as the key and 100% $font-stack as the value. As you can see, we have passed the variable here, which we know we can't do in CSS, but you can do in Sass. Then, this gets compiled into CSS so that it's translated:

```
body {
  font: 100% Helvetica, sans-serif;
  color: #333;
}
```

This allows us to change the value of a variable. If we want to change these fonts and have everything distributed site-wide, the change will go out site-wide wherever this variable is being used. Now, you may be wondering, regarding CSS, whether you can just create classes and then have your classes on the site, so why not change values inside the classes? Well, one thing about this is that when you want to make changes to classes, sometimes you may want to add a new value, and you will wind up in a situation where you're having to stack classes to make anything work. So, you have your original class, and now that you've done something different, you have to create one more class, so you have two classes now. It's getting a little more complex from that perspective. Here, however, we can basically write CSS as if we know it and are familiar with it, and then also write Sass all in the same file, in one place, and not really have to worry about going out to the CSS file. Instead, we just write it inside our SCSS file, which we're going to see in action in a little bit.

Let's go back into VS Code, where we're going to just perform some quick Sass variables, and then we're going to see how they are compiled once we have things running with Gulp displayed in our browser. In VS Code, first, let's go inside our scss folder and create a style.scss. Now, let's see the variables in action:

```
$font-stack: Helvetica, sans-serif;
$primary-color: #333;

body {
    font: 100% $font-stack;
    color: $primary-color;
}
```

Here, we have created a $font-stack variable and gave Helvetica and sans-serif as values. We also created one more variable called $primary-color and passed in #333 as the value. So, this was pretty straightforward. Next, we created a body tag and, inside that, we're going to define the font first. We'll keep it at 100%, and we're going to use our variable font-stack. We will then define the color and use the variable primary-color, put in our semicolons, and save it.

Now, when the `style.scss` file is compiled, we're going to have a `style.css` dropped under our `css` folder. As you can see, there's really not a lot of difference between defining these variables and what you can do with Sass. There's a lot more you can do, such as computations, use mixins, and so on, so it's quite powerful. However, this way, even if you're not going to use Sass and instead use straight CSS, you can do that too. The thing is, by working within this Sass file, you have the option to use Sass language. If you are sticking with CSS at first and then decide later that you really want to use Sass, you can go ahead and do so. Since you're working inside of this Sass file, just start using Sass right away. The reason we're not putting something into a `style.css` is because it's going to get overwritten with the compilation, so you'll see how that works in the following chapters. This is basically what Sass is. Next, we're going to get Gulp up and running.

Gulp

Now we're going to move on to building out our `gulpfile`. The first thing we want to do is put a `gulpfile` in the project area rather than the `src` file area. So, let's create a new file and call it `gulpfile.js`. The folder structure looks as follows:

The filename is important – you need to call it `gulpfile.js` so that Gulp can recognize it. Regarding our folder structure, this can be basically anything project-related or metadata-related for the forms of the parent folder, as shown previously. We have the `src` folder, where our actual web files are going to go, which are for displaying information on the website, or the kind of dependencies the website might need. This is how the folder structure is going to work as we go through our other different projects as well – this is going to kind of be a template.

Now, inside the `gulpfile`, we are going to create some variables to grab the dependencies that we're going to need. Let's look at the code:

```
var gulp = require('gulp')
var browserSync = require('browser-sync').create()
var sass = require('gulp-sass')

gulp.task('compile-sass', function(){
    return gulp.src(['node_modules/bootstrap/scss/bootstrap.scss',
    'src/scss/*.scss'])
    .pipe(sass())
    .pipe(gulp.dest('src/css'))
    .pipe(browserSync.stream())
})
})

gulp.task()
```

Here, we are going to use JavaScript syntax because we are in JavaScript files, so this ought to look familiar. We will start by creating variables. The first one is going to be `gulp`, and then we're going to create another variable and call it `browserSync`, do a `require` and get `browser-sync`, and then we want to call `create`. Then, we're going to create one more variable named `sass`, and this will require `gulp-sass`. Remember that we downloaded this earlier in our command line. Now, we have all the dependencies that we're going to need.

Next, we're going to create a `gulp.task`. Inside this task is going to be the compilation for our Sass, and we'll just call it `compile-sass` and create a function for this. This is where we're going to start chaining together some different functionalities. So, here, we're going to return out a few things. So, for the first one, we're going to create an array, so there's going to be two different sources in this array. The first one is going to be `node_modules/bootstrap/` and `scss/bootstrap.scss`. Let's put this inside single quotes. Alright, so we're going to have another location called `src/scss/*.scss`, which is going to be our own, so that's where we're going to be adding in our own CSS, or SCSS in this case, and save it. If you go and check out the first source and click on `bootstrap.scss`, you will see a bunch of imports that will be creating all the different dependencies for Bootstrap and its Sass files.

We have a few more things to do now. The next thing we're going to create is going to be a pipe, and basically the functionality, which is Sass. We are going to make another pipe with commands, so we're chaining everything together as we go. We're also going to do a `gulp.dest`. So, the way it works is it gets the files in *line 6* (see the following screenshot), compils them using Sass, and then drops them at the `src/css` destination, since the output is going to be a `.css` file. Then, we're going to make another pipe and finally call `browserSync`, the injection for the browser in this case, and stream it. This was our first task.

Next, we're going to move our JavaScript files so that we can do one more `gulp.task`:

```
gulp.task('move-js', function(){
    return gulp.src(['node_modules/bootstrap/dist/js/bootstrap.min.js',
    'node_modules/tether/dist/js/tether.min.js',
    'node_modules/jquery/dist/jquery.min.js'])
    .pipe(gulp.dest('src/js'))
    .pipe(browserSync.stream())
})
```

We're going to call this `move-js` and add another function. These follow similar types of patterns as we go through them, so again we will use `return gulp.src`, and this time we're going to take three different files and move them into our JavaScript folder, which is the one we created inside of our source files. This is going to be an array, and the first one I want is `node_modules/bootstrap/dist/js/`. Here, we're going to have `bootstrap.min.js`, which is our first one. We're going to do another similar one here, so we are going to have `node_modules/tether/dist/js/`, and we're going to get `tether.min.js`. There's one more we are going to make. It's going to be a jQuery, called `node_modules/jquery/dist/jquery.min.js`. Now let's start chaining these commands to get these moved over. Here, we're going to call a `gulp.dest` – we don't need to worry about compilations as in the earlier case, so the step with Sass is not there. It's going to go into our `js` folder, so then we're going to have one more pipe. Again, this is going to work with our injection into the browser, so we're going to call `browserSync.stream` and save.

Alright, so now we're going to have two more tasks. One is going to be another big task, and the other one is going to be just a single line:

```
gulp.task('launch-server', ['compile-sass'], function(){
    browserSync.init({
        server:'./src'
    })
    gulp.watch(['node_modules/bootstrap/scss/bootstrap.scss',
    'src/scss/*.scss'],
    ['compile-sass'])
```

```
        gulp.watch('src/*.html').on('change', browserSync.reload)
    })

    gulp.task('default', ['move-js','launch-server'])
```

As you can see, the next task that we created is going to launch our server – we will call it `launch-server` – and then we're going to have our `compile-sass` followed by a function where we will start the `browserSync` service and call the server from `./src`. Next, we're going to call a watch method. This is going to watch for any changes, and if that happens, it's going to go ahead and do the compilation and basically reload things. So, here, we're going to create an array and we're going to add the bootstrap files `node_modules/bootstrap/` and `scss/bootstrap.scss` and `src/scss/*.scss`. Then, we're going to do the compilation of `compile-sass`.

We then added one more watch method. This is going to reload our HTML. Here, we'll have a `src/*.html`, so if we make code changes to this file, we're going to call a change and call `browserSync.reload`. Now we are left with a single line code, and we are going to create one more gulp task, which will run everything. This will save us a lot of time and ensure that everything actually executes. As you can see, we have passed `move-js` and `launch-server`, and saved it.

Hello world example

In the last section, we completed our `gulpfile`, so now we will add comments to the different sections of the code. We're also going to try and give this a run. We may have to do a little bit of debugging because there's quite a bit of code we had written and a lot of opportunities to make some syntax errors. Here, we'll see what happens when we try to get this to run, so let's get started. Most of the code is fairly descriptive because of the names that were given. The first two tasks were easy to understand; what the function does is gather the locations we want to compile, runs them through the compiler, drops them at a destination, and then we have our browser injection. Now let's look at the third task where we are launching the server. We will have to add comments, as follows:

```
//run sass when server runs
//run server
//watch for any changes in src/scss folder and reload the browser
//watch for html changes
gulp.task('launch-server', ['compile-sass'], function(){
    browserSync.init({
        server:'./src'
    })
    gulp.watch(['node_modules/bootstrap/scss/bootstrap.scss',
```

```
    'src/scss/*.scss'],
    ['compile-sass'])
    gulp.watch('src/*.html').on('change', browserSync.reload)
})
```

So, if we make any changes there in our source code, those will be reflected in the browser, which is going to help our workflow quite a bit because we don't have to go back and relaunch the server, go and refresh the browser, or anything like that, and we're going to watch for HTML changes too. Here, we can see that we have the two watches, which means that we're watching for our Sass and then we're watching for HTML, and we're going to trigger browserSync.reload. Basically, if the source code changes, we're going to run the compile task compile-sass.

Now, let's add a comment to the last line of code:

```
//run gulp
//launch server and browser
//execute js task
gulp.task('default', ['move-js','launch-server'])
```

The comment in the preceding screenshot is self-explanatory. Now we are done, so let's try to run it. Type gulp in to the terminal and hit *Enter*. Here, we can see that the fonts are there. So, now, everything's running through our local versions:

Now, if we inspect it and go inside the <head> tag, you will see that everything is local:

```
<html lang="en">
  <head>
    <!-- Required meta tags -->
    <meta charset="utf-8">
    <meta name="viewport" content="width=device-width, initial-
      scale=1, shrink-to-fit=no">
    <!-- Bootstrap CSS -->
    <link rel="stylesheet" href="/css/bootstrap.css">
    <link rel="stylesheet" href="/css/style.css">
  </head>
```

If you scroll down, you will see the other links are also local:

```
<body>
  <h1>Hello, world!</h1>
  <!-- Optional JavaScript -->
  <!-- jQuery first, then Popper.js, then Bootstrap JS -->
  <script src="/js/jquery.min.js"></script>
  <script src="/js/tether.min.js"></script>
  <script src="/js/bootstrap.min.js"></script>
</body>
</html>
```

As you can see, Gulp is doing what we want it to do. We can also go back into VS Code and just take a look at what happened. So, we just ran the `gulp` command, and, as you can see, our tasks are running. It's giving us a time for how long it's taking for those to run (so fairly quickly), and then we have our server, which we're going to launch on port 3000:

Now, let's go and look at our folders as well:

You can see that we've got the three files that we wanted inside the `js` folder, and if we look in our `css` folder, we have our `bootstrap.css` and `style.css` files. The `style.css` file is the styling that was output through the compilation of the `style.scss` file. This is what it looks like:

```
body {
    font: 100% Helvetica, sans-serif;
    color: #333; }
```

If you match this code with the `style.css` code, it's the same, although the variables were replaced with their actual values and we have that output now.

Now you can try adding a background color to our `style.scss` file, as shown in the following screenshot:

```
$font-stack: Helvetica, sans-serif;
$primary-color: #333;
$bg-color: green;

body {
    font: 100% $font-stack;
    color: $primary-color;
    background: $bg-color;
}
```

Once you update the code and run it, you will see that the browser color has changed and that the changes are reflected in your CSS file:

Remember, the way that we've set this up is that we have the watches that are watching for any changes, and then we have the injection for the browser reload. We don't want to change `style.css` because it's going to get overwritten by whatever we're doing in `style.scss`. Again, we have the option to use Sass, and if we don't want to use it, we still need to stay inside the Sass file to do any kind of cascading style sheet work.

Alright, we have our **Hello, world!** working, we have Gulp working, and everything is up and running for our `HELLO_WORLD` project. This is actually going to be a template, so basically what that means is we can take everything except `node_modules`, zip it up, put it somewhere, and whenever we create a new project, we just unzip it – we'll have a project, and we'll be ready to go. So, that's the way it is going to work moving forward.

Summary

Let's quickly summarize what we've covered in this module. So, we got an introduction to Bootstrap 4 and what's new inside it. We've seen some great additions such as the Flexbox, the different changes they've done to the grids, we have new utilities that have come through, we have cards, and some of the new utilities such as Tether and the tool-tipping and the UI layout. Cards really are going to be a great UI feature that we can use and will probably look good on home pages or in sidebars. We also looked at our code editor, VS Code, which is made by Microsoft. It's a paired-down version of their IDE that's used to compile languages.

We also saw the integrated command-line tool and how to create a new project. Now, we have a template we can use going forward, which has got a particular folder structure. We've got Gulp for our task manager which we can go through, too – just execute Gulp and you'll have everything; the various files that we want will get moved, including JS and CSS, as well as the compilation of our Sass into CSS.

Then, we saw how Sass is being used inside Bootstrap. We saw a small demonstration of how Sass works and the precompilation of it into CSS as well, and then we had Gulp, our task manager, and created several tasks such as moving files for compiling Sass, and then, launched everything just by typing in the word gulp. Afterward we went through a simple Hello-World example. We got to see Gulp in action, so we made a change to our Sass to add that green background, and that was automatically detected with the watches that we had loaded up into the browser. This really made things very easy, with everything working in real-time with the code changes.

In the following chapters, we are going to start getting into the various projects that we're going to be working on throughout this book, with the help of the template that we created in this chapter.

Photosharing Website 3

In the last chapter, we saw the new features that were introduced in Bootstrap 4 and we also created a simple hello world example. In this chapter, we are going to build a photosharing website. To build this project, we are going to look into the following topics:

- Website layout
- Sass variables and CSS styling
- Creating the Contact and About pages
- Media breakpoints
- Installing Font Awesome
- Grid analysis

Building a menu

Now, we get to start on our first project. What I've done is taken our `hello_world` project and used it as our template for the first project. I copied the contents of the `hello_world` project into a folder named `P1`, for Project 1, and I've also copied in the `node_modules` so that I've got everything there that I need from `hello_world`, which is going to be a template going forward:

Using this as a template will make the project's startup time a little bit quicker. We also need to make sure that our Sass files are cleared, because we will be putting in our own variables for this project.

Before we start updating our `hello_world` template and shaping it into a photosharing website, I want you to get a rough idea of what we are going to build. The following is a screenshot of the photosharing website's home page. There are obviously more features added to it, so we will try to closely match this with its function and appearance:

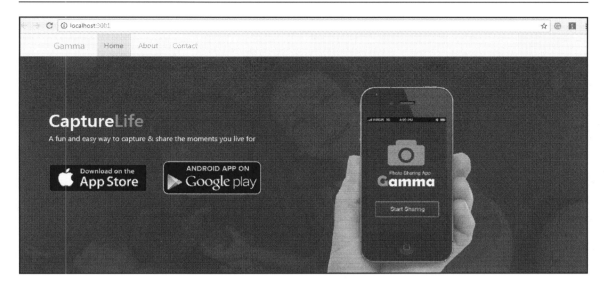

Let's go into our `index.html`. Here, we are going to modify the section under the `<body>` tag. We are going to replace the `Hello, world!` text inside the body with the following code:

```
<body>
  <nav class="navbar navbar-expand-md navbar-light bg-light fixed-top">
    <div class="container">
      <a class="navbar-brand em-text" href="index.html">Gamma</a>
      <button class="navbar-toggler" type="button" data-
      toggle="collapse" data-target="#navbarsExample09" aria-
      controls="#navbarsExample09" aria-expanded="false" aria-
      label="Toogle navigation">
        <span class="navbar-toggler-icon"></span>
      </button>
    </div>
```

The first thing we're going to do is create a navbar, and inside of it we're going to have a few classes. The first one is going to be our `navbar`, which is basically the root class that we want to have some navbar functionality. Next, we have `navbar-expand-md` to make our navbar expand out, and we're going to have it triggered on a medium size. We're going to add `navbar-light`, which provides colors, and we're going to have a background color, `bg-light`. Finally, we're going to fix it to the top. This is pretty straightforward in regard to what exactly is happening here. If you save and run it, there's not really going to be anything to see yet, so we're going to add a little bit more code and then we're going to start seeing the progress unfold on our website.

Next, we're going to add a `div` tag, which is going to have a class called `container` that wraps up our content. For Bootstrap, you don't necessarily have to have content wrapped inside a container – it's okay if things are outside of the container; it completely depends on your design. In this case, we have different backgrounds that will go on the website and as the site gets built out, you'll see more of what's happening. Some backgrounds may stretch to 100% within their container, and some go on behind the container and stretch to 100% as well. So, as this gets going, we'll see some of that in action.

Now, we're going to have a class called `navbar-brand`. `navbar-brand` is actually used for branding, and is mainly used for company names or a logo. Sometimes, you'll want to do some styling against it to get your own kinds of customizations coming through. So, we have `em-text`, which is going to be a custom class, so once we get into our Sass file, we'll see more on how that's done. We have named the link `Gamma`, so you will be redirected to the `index.html` page.

Then, we are going to create a button with the `navbar-toggler` class. This is going to toggle the menu depending on what's happening with the sizing of the browser and its responsiveness. We're going to have a `data-target`, which targets a section on a page, named `#navbarsExample09`. Next, we have the `aria-controls`. Here, `aria` stands for accessible rich internet application, and it's for accessibility. So, we'll point that to the same place as well. We'll also have `aria-expanded` – no expansion in this case, hence we will keep it `false`—and then we'll have `aria-label` set to `Toggle navigation`, which is again for accessibility reasons. Now, we have to create an icon, which is going to be the familiar hamburger icon, so we will add a class called `navbar-toggler-icon` and save it. So at this point, we're going to go ahead and type `gulp` in the terminal and run our website. As you can see, we have the hamburger icon and our menu here with the brand **Gamma**, which is clickable:

There's nothing much to really see at this point, but let's go ahead and continue expanding this page out.

Now, we will create the other sections in the menu, that is, the `Home`, `About`, and `Contact` sections, which are going to be similar to what we had with `Gamma`. The code is as follows:

```
<div class="collapse navbar-collapse" id="navbarsExample09">
  <ul class="nav navbar-nav mr-auto">
    <li class="active"><a href="index.html" class="nav-link">Home</a>
    </li>
```

```
        <li><a href="about.html" class="nav-link">About</a></li>
        <li><a href="contact.html" class="nav-link">Contact</a></li>
    </ul>
  </div>
```

So, we will add a `div` class inside the `div` class we just created, and this is going to be `collapse navbar-collapse`. We will give it an ID name of `navbarsExample09`. This is the target that we mentioned earlier in the `button` tag. Now, we will have a `ul` class set to `nav navbar-nav`. So, currently the hamburger menu is in a collapsed state. When it expands, you'll see the different elements for `About`, `Contact`, and `Home` appearing vertically once you open the hamburger icon. Currently, it is horizontal. We have an `mr-auto`, which stands for margin right auto. So, you're applying an auto margin. You also have an `ml-auto`, so you can have a margin left. Next, we will list our elements that will link to each page. So, the first one is an active element, which is going to be the `Home`, and we link it to `index.html`. We will then add `class="nav-link"` for styling. Now, we can go ahead and copy this same line of code for `About` and `Contact`, except for the `active` class, which we have to remove. Also, make sure that the reference is made correct to their respective pages, which is `about.html` and `contact.html`. When we run the file now, you will see the following output in your browser:

We have more functionalities to add as we progress. In the next section, we will continue building out some of this main content area and the footer as well.

Footer

We're going to continue with our `index.html` and, at this point, we're going to go ahead and create the `footer` section, which is going to be reused throughout our other pages. Let's go ahead and add `footer` tags just above our scripts. Let's look at the `footer` code:

```
<footer>
  <div class="container">
    <div class="row">
      <div class="col-lg-6 col-md-7 col-sm-12">
        <ul>
          <li><a href="#">Home</a></li>
          <li><a href="#">About</a></li>
          <li><a href="#">Contact</a></li>
          <li><a href="#">Privacy Policy</a></li>
        </ul>
```

```
        </div>
      </div>
    </div>
  </footer>
```

So, inside the `footer` tag, we're going to create a `class="container"` to contain all of the footer content. We will then add a `<div class="row">` to set a grid system. For the grid, we're going to have our column, `col-lg-6`. In Bootstrap 4, just in regard to the grid itself, there're basically five breakpoints. So, we have our `xl`, `lg` that we're using here, `md`, `sm`, and `xs`. `sm` is going to start at `768px`, and `xs` is going to start at `576px`. Now that we have our `lg` for large devices, we're going to add columns for medium and extra small devices, which are `col-md-7` and `col-xs-12`. Now, we can go ahead and create our page links, and those are going to go inside of an unordered list. We'll start with our list items – there's nothing active in this case—and we're going to just set the references to # so there won't be any active links, but they're going to mimic it, which is really all we need. So, we'll have a `Home`, `About`, `Contact`, and also a `Privacy Policy`. These aren't going to go in the main menu, but are going to be down at the footer. Let's save, refresh the browser, and view the output:

We can see some of the footer information starting to come through. Let's go ahead and continue building on that.

The next thing we're going to do is create another `div` that's going to be for our copyright, `All Rights Reserved`, and it's going have its own row. So, we will copy the same structure as the columns we just created and update it. Let's look at the code now:

```
<div class="col-lg-6 col-md-7 col-sm-12">
  <p>Copyright &copy;2018, All Rights Reserved</p>
</div>
```

Inside the paragraph tag, we wrote `Copyright`, and we're going to add `&copy;` for the `Copyright` symbol, followed by the year `2018, All Rights Reserved`, and then save it. Let's take a look at how that is shaping up:

So, we can see that it is not exactly where we want it to be; it should go to the bottom. Again, we're just watching this develop as we're creating and adding different code.

Jumbotron

In this section, we are going to build a jumbotron, which looks something similar to the following screenshot:

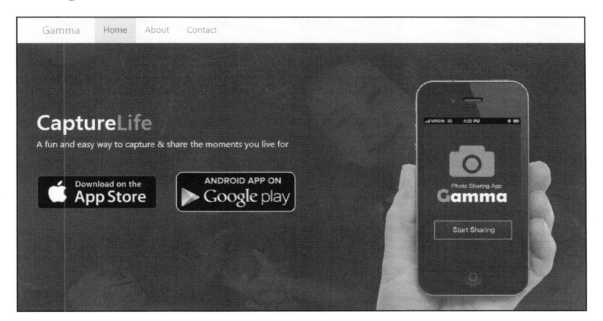

We will require images from here onward. You can use any image you want to design your website. You will have to place the images inside the img folder under the src folder, as shown in the following screenshot:

We're moving away from the navigation now. We will add a new div tag, which will come before the footer code and after the nav code. This div is going to be for our jumbotron. Inside the jumbotron, we're going to put our container, and then inside of the container, we will have our row as follows:

```html
<div class="jumbotron">
  <div class="container">
    <div class="row">
      <div class="col-lg-6">
        <h1>Capture<span class="em-text">Life</span></h1>
        <p>A fun and easy way to capture & share the moments you live
        for</p>
```

```
        <a href="#"><img class="app-btn" src="img/icon_app_store.png">
        </a>
        <a href="#"><img class="app-btn"
        src="img/icon_google_play.png"></a>
      </div>
      <div class="col-lg-6">
        <img class="showcase-img" src="img/site_phone.png">
      </div>
    </div>
  </div>
</div>
```

Alright, so we're going to create a large column. It's going to be a 6 on the sizing, so we'll have class="col-lg-6", which is basically going to split the jumbotron area in two halves. Now, on the left side, we're going to add some text and images from Google Play and Apple Store. These two images or logos will act as links, but they won't be active, so we will add # in href.

Now, let's create a div for the right-hand side. Let's create a class for the large column and add an image called showcase-img. The code is pretty self-explanatory. Let's save and run the file, and we will see the following output:

So, there's still some styling left to do, which is the same with footer. Now, we will go ahead and create the middle section that comes between the jumbotron and the footer.

Main content sections

Until now, we have seen navigation, the footer, and a jumbotron. Now, we will be looking to fill in the middle area that lies between the jumbotron and the footer. We still have to work on these sections, as they are still not what we want because some of our styling that we're referencing is not there yet. We will fix this after we create the middle area. The middle area will again be divided into two sections. The first section will have some images and text, and it will be divided into three blocks as follows:

Lorem Ipsum

Why do we use it? It is a long established fact that a reader will be distracted by the readable content of a page when looking at its layout. The point of using Lorem Ipsum is that it has a more-or-less normal distribution of letters, as opposed to using 'Content here, content here', making it look

Read More

Lorem Ipsum

Why do we use it? It is a long established fact that a reader will be distracted by the readable content of a page when looking at its layout. The point of using Lorem Ipsum is that it has a more-or-less normal distribution of letters, as opposed to using 'Content here, content here', making it look

Read More

Lorem Ipsum

Why do we use it? It is a long established fact that a reader will be distracted by the readable content of a page when looking at its layout. The point of using Lorem Ipsum is that it has a more-or-less normal distribution of letters, as opposed to using 'Content here, content here', making it look

Read More

The second section will come below the first section and it will have the following features:

The middle and the `feature` section code will go between the `jumbotron` and `feature`, as follows:

```
<section id="feature">
  <div class="container">
    <div class="row">
      <div class="col-lg-5">
        <h1>Gamma Features</h1>
        <ul>
          <li><i class="fa fa-check" aria-hidden"true"></i>Donec
            pulvinar</li>
          <li><i class="fa fa-check" aria-hidden"true"></i>It is a long
            established fact that a reader</li>
          <li><i class="fa fa-check" aria-hidden"true"></i>Pulvinar
            ante</li>
          <li><i class="fa fa-check" aria-hidden"true"></i>Eusmod
            mauris rutrum</li>
        </ul>
      </div>
      <div class="col-lg-4 offset-lg-2">
        <img class="big-logo" src="img/logo.png">
      </div>
    </div>
  </div>
</section>
```

Let's start coding the middle section. The first thing we're going to do is add our container, and then we're going to have a row. We will then add a column of size `col-lg-4`:

```
<section id="middle">
  <div class="container">
    <div class="row">
        <div class="col-lg-4">
            <img src="img/demo1.jpg" class="demo">
```

```
        <h2>Lorem Ipsum</h2>
        <p>Why do we use it?
            It is a long established fact that a reader will be
            distracted by the readable content of a page when looking
            at its layout. The point of using Lorem Ipsum is that it
            has a more-or-less normal distribution of letters, as
            opposed to using 'Content here, content here', making it
            look
        </div>
      </div>
    </div>
  </section>
```

For our first row, we're going to add an image called demo1.jpg, and it's going to be a class="demo". We will then add a heading and name it Lorem Ipsum, and follow it with some text taken from https://lipsum.com/. Let's save and check the output. It looks as follows:

So, we have our picture of a phone and the Lorem Ipsum text. Now, we can do our **Read More**, which is going to be an `href`. We're going to use a class from Bootstrap. So, it's going to be `btn` and `btn-outline-secondary`, and that is just a particular type of button, so if you look at the different ones available, you'll probably find something that you like. The `role` we are going to use is `button`. We'll see the visual aspect of this shortly, but before that, we will do the same for the remaining two sections. We will just copy and paste the code that we just wrote and only update the image and text. Once done, you will see the output, which should be something like this:

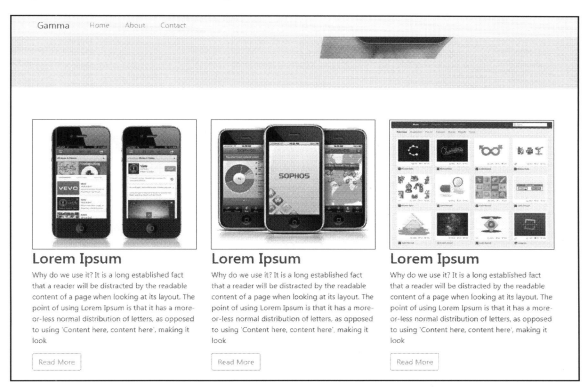

Now, let's move on to the `feature` section. We're going to create a `div` again of the `container` class, and then we will have another row, because we're going to have columns that we're going to set. So, this is going to be `class="col-lg-5"`. There's that odd number again, just based on what makes the grid look best. So, we're going to have Gamma Features, and then below that we'll have our unordered list, as shown earlier in this section. Let's look at the code:

```
<section id="feature">
  <div class="container">
    <div class="row">
      <div class="col-lg-5">
        <h1>Gamma Features</h1>
        <ul>
          <li><i class="fa fa-check" aria-hidden"true"></i>Donec
          pulvinar</li>
          <li><i class="fa fa-check" aria-hidden"true"></i>It is a long
          established fact that a reader</li>
          <li><i class="fa fa-check" aria-hidden"true"></i>Pulvinar
          ante</li>
          <li><i class="fa fa-check" aria-hidden"true"></i>Eusmod
          mauris rutrum</li>
        </ul>
      </div>
    </div>
  </div>
</section>
```

So, we have created an unordered list, which will consist of classes that are coming from Font Awesome, which we don't actually have a reference to. We're going to look at that a little later on, as we're just adding in the classes for now. So, we have our `aria-hidden`, which is going to be `true`. After that, add some Lorem Ipsum text. Do the same for the next three in the list.

So, we have one more image that we're going to use, a `div` that closes out that section there with our unordered list, and we're going to add another class, which is going to be a `col-lg-4`. We're going to use `offset-lg-2` for this. So, this offset here just depends on what exactly you're doing with your grid, so it may make one column shift over from another column, for example, and that's what's going on in this case. Alright, so this is our code:

```
<div class="col-lg-4 offset-lg-2">
  <img class="big-logo" src="img/logo.png">
</div>
```

We have our `big-logo` class and an image of the logo. Let's go to our site and see what it looks like:

So, a basic skeleton layout is what's going on at this point. As the styling comes in, you'll see this starting to tighten up a bit and start looking more like the site we planned to build. We still have a little bit to go as far as the CSS is concerned, but what we can do, since we've got this index page created content-wise, layout-wise, we're going to move into getting these style sheets active and start having the references come through into the `index.html`, which will make it look closer to the finished product fairly quickly. All of the content that we really need to put into this `index.html` is already present. So in the next section, what we're going to do is see this starting to form up into the final product, at least for the Home page.

Starting Sass build out

Now, we're getting to the point where we are ready to start attaching our CSS reference to this page, and we're going to see some differences in the way it's going to look because of that. So, this means that we're getting into creating our Sass file and building that out. Gulp is then going to run behind the scenes automatically when it detects those changes, do the pre-processing, and deploy that Sass code as CSS into our CSS file. So, right now, there are a few things on the `index.html` page that we want to update, but we need not worry about them as the CSS is going to come in and start fixing all of this.

Now that we know our layout is pretty well intact, we can proceed with our Sass build out. There's quite a bit of Sass that we're going to be working on here, so we're going to start off by creating a few variables. For that, we are going to define some variables for colors:

```
$very-dark-gray :#555;
$very-light-gray :#e7e7e7;
$dark-cyan :#1caa98;
$very-dark-blue :#1b222a;
```

You will basically get a hint of what the colors are. We're going to have four kinds of colors. One thing we want to do is go ahead and add some styling to the body with the `body` tag, and also the `navbar`. So, let's go ahead and see what the code looks like:

```
body {
    padding-top:50px;
}

.navbar {
    padding:0;
}

.nav.navbar-nav {
    .nav-link{
        padding:0.85rem 1rem;
    }
    .active{
        .nav-link{
            color:$very-dark-gray;
            background:$very-light-gray;
        }
    }
}
```

For the body, we're just getting into some CSS, and we're going to use `padding-top:50px`. Now, we're going to add styles to `navbar`. As you can see, we are hitting the class coming right out of Bootstrap. We're going to use `padding:0`, which is just a customization of how we want this thing to look. You can actually play around with these to your liking regarding how you might want your padding to appear, but this is just going to give you basic knowledge of how to do that. Then, we're going to work on the `nav-link`, and for that we're going to use padding too. It's going to be `0.85` and we're getting into `rem` so that we're not making use of pixels here, following Bootstrap 4's best practices. We're still dealing with the links, so let's set the `active` state. We'll go back in with our `nav-link` again so that we get to use our colors. It's going to be `very-dark-gray`, and then we'll set the background to `very-light-gray`. So, let's go ahead and save it, and then scroll down to our integrated terminal. You're going to see some differences in the terminal once you save. When you save, it preprocesses, and you will see that the `style.css` file has updated. The code is now translated fully into CSS. Now, if we go back out to the site, we will be able to see what it looks like:

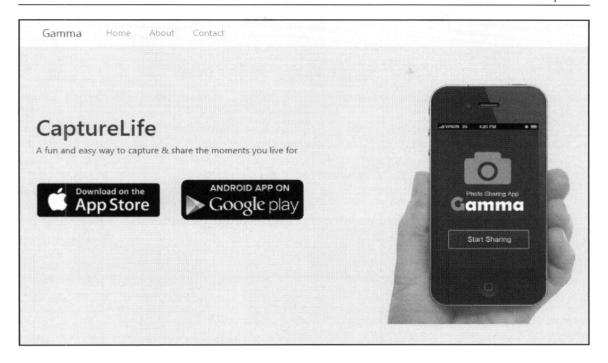

So, you can see that the menu looks a bit different. As we click on the various menu items, they should highlight and change. The menu is still incomplete, as clicking on About and Contact won't take you anywhere. Alright, let's continue in our Sass and close the style sheet since we don't want to be in there.

Now, we're going to hit the brand on the navbar:

```
.navbar-brand {
    padding:.65rem;
}

.em-text {
    color:$dark-cyan !important;
}

.col-lg-4 {
    margin-bottom: 20px;
}
```

We are going to add padding to the `.navbar-brand`, which is going to be `.65rem`. Now, let's change the class that we had inside of our `index.html`, which was `em-text`. Let's add `color:$dark-cyan` and a space. Now, what we want to do is ensure that this is going to override—we don't want to have Sass coming in. This is using colors, so that's why we are using `!important` here. So, when do we use `!important`? If there's something inside of the framework that you need to override, or if you want to use it yourself, `!important` can help in identifying which one that is. So, if you're doing something and you notice, for example, a color that you're setting is not coming through, and it's still using the Bootstrap color, that's an indication that you may want to override with an `!important`. Okay, so that's our `em-text` class. Now, what we're going to do is work on our `col-lg-4` and set some margins. These are just minor customizations, but how do you know which ones have to be customized? It just depends on the look you're going after, so it's kind of trial and error to get it to look the way you want it to. So, since I've already been through this, I know this requires a little bit of padding. If you remember, those photos we had in that middle section were all crammed together, so I'm going to separate them a little bit. Now, let's work on the `section` tag, where we want to do some padding as well, because if you remember, the last time we saw everything it was pretty crammed:

```
section {
    padding:40px 0 40px 0;
}
```

So, if you save and have a look at the site, you will see the spacing between the jumbotron and the middle section, and also between the middle section and the `feature` section. Now, we're going to deal with our jumbotron. The code is as follows:

```
.jumbotron{
    background: $very-dark-blue url(../img/site_showcase_bg.jpg) no-
repeat top center;
    color: white;
    height: 500px;
    overflow:hidden;
}
```

There are four different changes we're going to make inside of our Sass. The first one is going to be the background. We're going to go with `very-dark-blue`, and I'm going to use the variable that we created and add a space after that. Now, we are going to reference the `site_showcase_bg.jpg` image in the `img` folder because remember we've got to back out of our `sass` folder, or in this case we're actually going to be in the `css`. Either way, it's the same difference—you've got to go up one level, which is what those two dots are for. We don't want this to repeat. Then, we're going with top center for the alignment. After that, we fix the height on this, which is `500px` in our case, and the `overflow`, which we will set to `hidden`. Let's go have a look at the jumbotron:

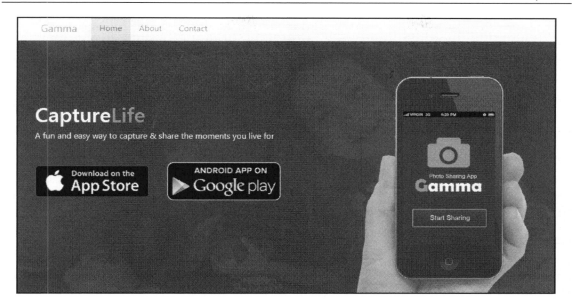

So as you can see, we are making some good progress on the jumbotron. This is starting to look good and shape up quite well. The menu is there. We still have a little bit more work to do on the jumbotron, but after we're finished, we can then start moving into the other areas.

Completing Sass for index

In the last section, we left off with starting to do some styling on our jumbotron. There are a few more things we're going to do on the jumbotron, mainly adding margins and making it appear much better than how it looks now:

```
.jumbotron h1 {
    margin-top: 60px;
}
.jumbotron p {
    margin-bottom: 40px;
}
.jumbotron img.app-btn {
    width:40%;
    margin-right:30px;
}
.jumbotron img.showcase-img{
    width:75%;
}
```

As you can see, the code is self-explanatory. As mentioned earlier, it's a trial and error method to see what components of the website look like when it comes to styling. We have added a style to the heading, `Capture Life`, the text below it, the Google Play and Apple Store images, and finally the image on the right-hand side of the jumbotron.

Once you make these changes to the jumbotron code, you can inspect the elements and play with the margin and widths you have added by checking and unchecking them to get an idea of how the layout has changed:

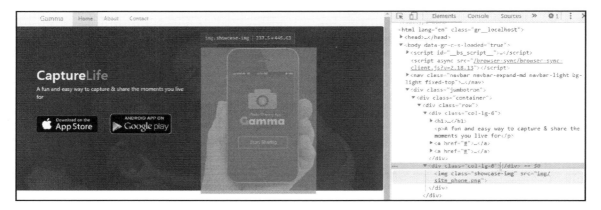

 You can see how the jumbotron looks now and you have the code that follows, which can be seen after right-clicking on the screen and selecting **Inspect Element**. On the bottom-right side, you have the styles that we've added. You can uncheck and check each parameter to see the difference.

Now, we're going to do some modifications to our section for the feature, so let's go ahead and add some styles:

```
section#feature{
    background:$dark-cyan;
    color:white;
    padding:40px;
    overflow:auto;
}
```

Here, the first thing we want to do is add the dark cyan color on the background. We will make use of our variable here, that is, `$dark-cyan`. Our color is going to be white, and we're going to have some padding. This is going to be all-around padding. Here, `overflow` is going to be `auto`. Then, we'll save this, which is going to process and generate our CSS. If we go back now and look at the `feature` section on the site, you should see the following output:

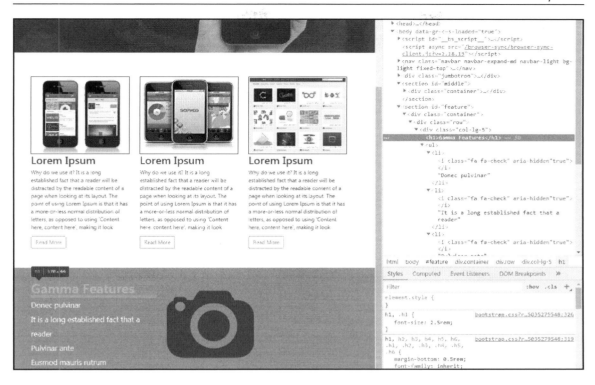

Here, you can see that the cyan color is certainly coming through now and that we're starting to get some pretty good styling in place. You can highlight the `section`, as shown in the preceding screenshot, and check or uncheck the parameters to see the effects they have.

Now, let's target the unordered list in the `feature` section. The code for that would be as follows:

```
section#feature ul li{
    font-size:22px;
    list-style:none;
    line-height:2.0em;
}

section#feature ul {
    padding:0;
    margin:0;
}
```

First, we target the unordered list items. Here, we're going to target their `font-size`, so we're going to make them quite big—let's set it to `22`. Regarding `list-style`, we're going to go with none, and then we're going to do a line height of `2.0em`. So, we have done quite a bit of customization here. You can save the file here and go and check the changes are reflected on the site. Okay, now we're going to work on the unordered list itself. What we're going to do is remove the padding and the margin, so we just want to target the `ul`, and we're going to use `padding:0` and `margin:0`. Let's see the output:

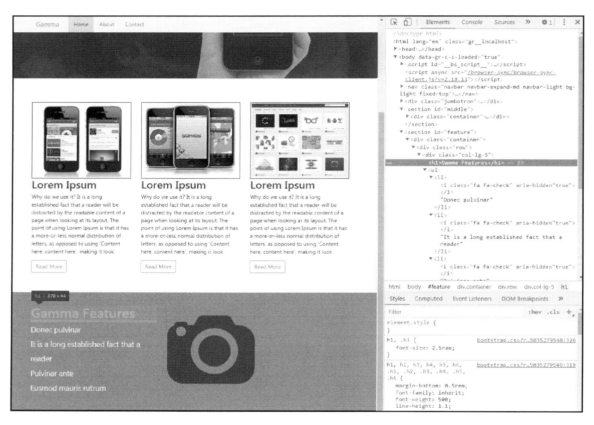

If I click on the margin, as shown in the preceding screenshot, you won't see much effect, but just adding that there reassures us that there's not going to be any margin. So, Bootstrap didn't have an effect, the browser didn't have an effect, but what's to say a different browser won't have some kind of margin that it's going to apply? For now, that's about all we can do on the index. However, there's still quite a bit more Sass to build out. I don't want to go ahead and start building Sass out for the other pages since we can't actually look at the effect that it's going to have, so what we're going to do is start adding these other pages, and then we'll come back and start adding the remaining Sass that's going to affect those pages. So in the next section, we'll get into our Contact and About pages, so that when we click the menu items we'll be able to see how the styling and the menu changes, and then we'll also have some new pages that we can work with.

Creating the Contact page

In the last section, we look at fixed spacing issues in text and images, especially in jumbotron. What we're going to do now is add our Contact page, so let's go back to our VS Code. What we want is to get into the root of the src folder and add a file called contact.html. We will now copy and paste the content in the index.html from our very first Hello, world!. So, every time you start a new project, you can use this template code and get started with new page creation. So, obviously there are a few changes we're going to make in here to suit the current project. The first thing we're going to do is to remove the Hello, world! heading that we created. Next, we will get our nav. We're going to use everything inside of the nav tags in our index.html file. Copy the entire content in the nav tag and paste it inside the body tag of the contact.html page.

So, within the nav tag, we are going to change the active class. Earlier, the index.html page was active, so now we will remove that and make the contact.html page active, as shown in the following screenshot:

```
<div class="collapse navbar-collapse" id="navbarsExample09">
  <ul class="nav navbar-nav mr-auto">
      <li><a href="index.html" class="nav-link">Home</a></li>
      <li><a href="about.html" class="nav-link">About</a></li>
      <li class="active"><a href="contact.html" class="nav-
      link">Contact</a></li>
  </ul>
</div>
```

Next, we want a title on the Contact page. We will be adding that below the nav. We will be using a section tag for that and we will give it an id="title-bar". Here is the code:

```
<section id="title-bar">
    <div class="container">
        <div class="row">
            <div class="col-lg-12">
                <h1>Contact Us</h1>
            </div>
        </div>
    </div>
</section>
```

Inside the section tag, we will have a container class followed by row, and then we will have the column set to col-lg-12 and the h1 heading tag for Contact Us. Save it and let's check what the Contact page looks like:

It looks pretty good now. Let's go ahead and add some styling to the title bar before we go ahead and work on the content for this page. Here is the code:

```
section#title-bar{
    padding:0;
    margin:0;
    height:80px;
    background: $dark-cyan;
    color:white;
}
```

Basically, we have removed the padding, added a height, and set the background color, dark-cyan, for our title bar. Let's see how it looks now:

Here, you can see the difference after we added some styles to it. Let's go ahead and create the main content for our Contact page. We will have to create one more section for this main content, which will follow the `title-bar` section.

The following screenshot is a sample of what we are planning to build:

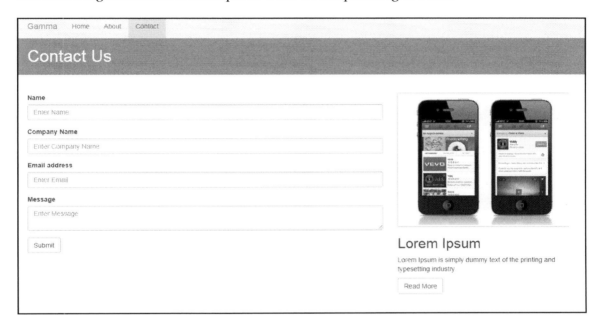

On the left, we have some form fields and on the right, we have an image and text. The form fields takes two-thirds of the main content are, and the image and text on the right side takes one-third of the area, so we will create the grid system accordingly. The following code shows the grid layout of the main content section of `contact.html`:

```
<section id="contact">
    <div class="container">
        <div class="row">
            <div class="col-lg-8">
            </div>
            <div class="col-lg-4">
            </div>
        </div>
    </div>
</section>
```

Now, we will start working on the form fields. We'll start off by adding a `form` tag, and then we're going to have a class called `form-group`, as shown in the following screenshot:

```
<form><div class="form-group">
    <label>Name</label>
    <input type="text" class="form-control" placeholder="Enter Name">
</div>
```

We will add styles to the `form-group` class later, but before that, we will create the layout. We will add a `label` called `Name`. The `input` tag is basically an input box and will take `text` as input. We also have our `form-control` class from Bootstrap, which we are adding for style. Since the input field is going to be empty, we will add a `placeholder` for **Enter Name**. Now, let's save this and check what it looks like on the site:

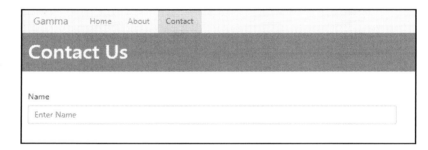

There you go! We will now create the remaining form fields in a similar way. We will copy and paste the code for the `Name` field and update it as per our requirements.

So, the remaining code will look as follows:

```
<div class="form-group">
    <label>Company Name</label>
    <input type="text" class="form-control" placeholder="Enter
    Company Name">
</div>
<div class="form-group">
    <label>Email address</label>
    <input type="text" class="form-control" placeholder="Enter
    Email">
</div>
<div class="form-group">
    <label>Message</label>
    <textarea class="form-control" placeholder="Enter Message">
    </textarea>
</div>
</form>
```

Now, we have added fields for `Company Name`, `Email address`, and `Message`. The code for `Company Name` and `Email address` are similar to `Name`, as we saw earlier; however, there is a slight change in the code for `Message`. Instead of the `input` tag, we will have `textarea`. Basically, the input box has been changed here, as the `Message` field will take more text than the other fields. We will also remove `type="text"`, then close the `textarea` tag and save it. Before we go ahead and see what it looks like on the website, we will create the `Submit` button as well.

The `Submit` button is going to go outside of the `div` and before closing the `form` tag. Here is the code:

```
<button type="submit" class="btn btn-outline-secondary">Submit</button>
```

So, we have a button with the `type` as `submit`. We'll get the styling right out of Bootstrap on this button, so we're going to have `btn btn-outline-secondary`, display the name of the button as **Submit**, and save it. Let's look at the output:

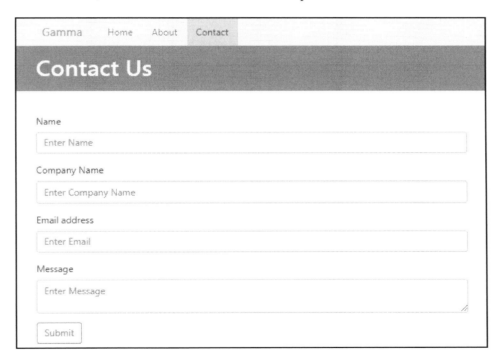

There are still some spacing issues compared to the sample we saw at the start of this section. We will come back later and fix this. Now, we will move on to the other side and add the image, text, and Read More button.

So, the code for the right-hand side of the page will be as follows:

```
<div class="col-lg-4">
    <img src="img/demo1.jpg" class="demo">
    <h2>Lorem Ipsum</h2>
    <p>It is a long established fact that a reader will be distracted
by the readable content of a page when looking at its layout.</p>
    <a href="#" class="btn btn-outline-secondary" role="button">Read
More</a>
</div>
```

We started with our `img src`, which is going to be the path inside of the `img/` folder. It's going to be `demo1.jpeg` and the class is going to be `demo`. Then, we're going to have a heading, `h2`, which will have `Lorem Ipsum` text, and below the heading we will add a paragraph of text, where you can put anything you want. Now, let's go ahead to our **Read More** button and add a class from Bootstrap. We've used these before. We going to use the same one we used previously, but just giving a faded role to the UI so that it's not so prevalent, but still visible and you know what to do with them. Finally, give it the role of a button. Let's save it and look at the page now:

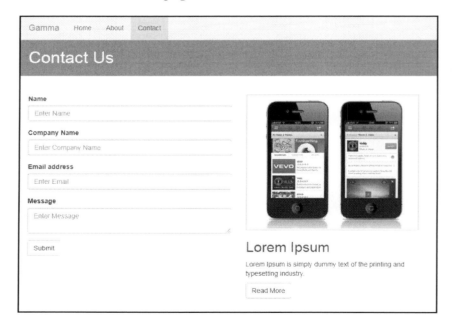

As you can see, there's a little bit of styling that needs to go on for everything to align, and we'll see how to do that in the next section. Once we do these minor adjustments to the `Contact` page, we'll then start moving on to the `About` page.

Building the content section of the Contact page

In the last section, we left off with our Contact page. Right now, this page doesn't actually have a footer, so we're going to add that. Then, we're going to add some styling for this page and particularly for the footer, and once that is complete, we can move on to our About page. So, let's go ahead, go into our VS Code, and grab the footer, which we wrote earlier in the index.html file. So, if we copy the footer code from index.html paste it into our contact.html file, and save it, you should see the footer added at the bottom of the page. So, to style the footer, we are going to go into our Sass file, that is, the style.scss file, and add a few different attributes for the footer:

```
footer {
    background:lighten(black,20%);
    color:white;
    padding: 30px 0 20px 0;
}
footer li {
    float:left;
    padding: 0 10px 0 10px;
    list-style:none;
}
```

So, the first thing we are going to do is make the background color lighten, and black is going to be 20%. We will change the color to white and also add padding. You can see that sometimes we are using px and a lot of Bootstrap. For now, this is rem and em. It's fine to use px. When you're dealing with fonts, you're going to be using em. Next, we're going to remove the bullet points in the footer section. As you can see in the preceding code, float:left will make the links in the footer section appear side by side instead of as a list. Next, we have added padding and finally, to remove the bullets, we have added list-style:none.

Now, since the background is black, the links don't seem visible enough, so we need to make the color white and also the copyright text float right. Here is the code:

```
footer a {
    color: white;
}
footer p {
    float:right;
}
```

Save the code and run it. You will see that the footer section has changed a lot compared to how it was before we started this section:

Now, looking at our site, we need to do a little bit of work on the picture on the `Contact` page. Let's go ahead and fix it. If you inspect the image in the browser, you will see the name of the image and the `class="demo"`. This is an easy way to figure out the details, as shown in the following screenshot:

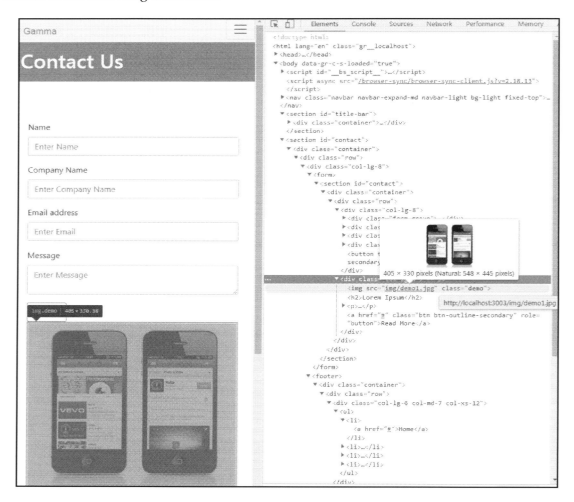

We are going work on that demo class now. Here is the code:

```
img.demo {
    width:100%;
    padding: 3px;
    border: 1px solid darken(black,80%);
}
```

Let's go to our style.scss file and write this code below the jumbotron, which is img.showcase as a best practice. So we add img.demo, which we will give a width of 100%, a padding of 3px, and a border of 1px solid. We're going to darken it by 80% and save it. So, let's rerun gulp in the terminal. Let's go back and check out what our Contact page now looks like. The following is the output:

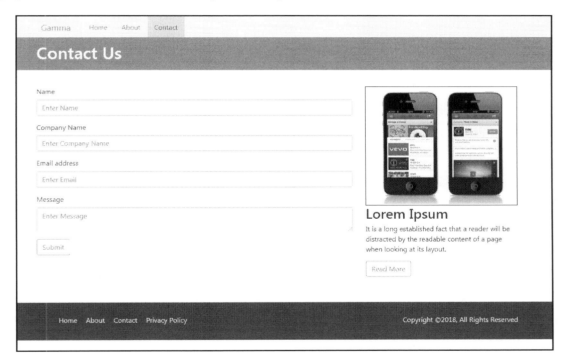

Now, as you can see in the preceding screenshot, we have to fix the **Contact Us** title, so let's go ahead and do that. If you go and check the contact.html file, this part falls under the section with id="title-bar". Now, let's go to our style.scss file and add the styling:

```
section#title-bar h1{
    margin: 1rem 0;
}
```

Adding a margin with 1rem and 0 should fix this problem. Let's save and check the Contact page:

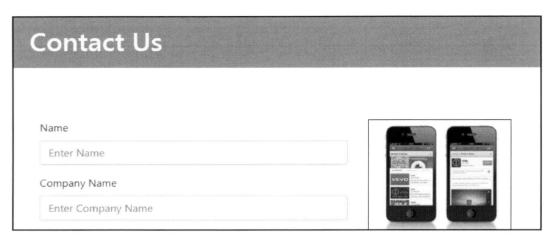

There it is! The title looks much better now. Now that we are done with the Contact page, let's go and create our About page.

Creating the About page

We will go into our VS Code now and add an About page. Let's create a new file called about.html, similar to what we did for the contact.html file. We are going to copy the header, footer, and the nav code from the index.html file and paste them into our about.html file. Please make sure that the code is pasted at the right places, as we did earlier for the Contact page. We will require a title-bar as well for our About page, which we can get from the contact.html file. The only thing to update is the name of the title-bar. Instead of Contact Us, change it to About Gamma:

```
<section id="title-bar">
    <div class="container">
        <div class="row">
            <div class="col-lg-12">
                <h1>About Gamma</h1>
            </div>
        </div>
    </div>
</section>
```

Another thing that we have to change is making the About page link active. Here is the code:

```
<div class="collapse navbar-collapse" id="navbarsExample09">
   <ul class="nav navbar-nav mr-auto">
       <li><a href="index.html" class="nav-link">Home</a></li>
       <li class="active"><a href="about.html" class="nav-
       link">About</a></li>
       <li><a href="contact.html" class="nav-link">Contact</a></li>
   </ul>
</div>
```

If we go back to our site and check the About page, you should see something like this:

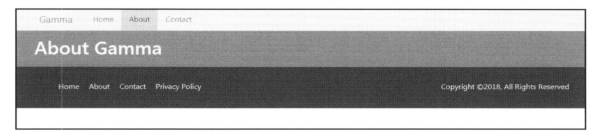

Now, we have to work on the middle content. Similar to our Contact page, we will also divide the About page's middle area into two columns, one of size 8 and other of size 4:

```
<section id="about">
    <div class="container">
        <div class="row">
            <div class="col-lg-8">
            </div>
            <div class="col-lg-4">
            </div>
        </div>
    </div>
</section>
```

We have just created the basic layout of the page. In the next section, we will continue building out the About page.

Building the content section of the About page

We're moving into building out the content section for our About page. If we take a look at the target site, as shown in the following screenshot, we have these collapsible groups, which we're going to have to build in and are part of an accordion class. We're going to do some styling against it because it comes out of Bootstrap 4. Here, we're going to use the base class and we're going to apply our own kind of styling, but there's not really too much going on. We're already familiar with the right-hand side, so we are just going to add in some text and an image, and build out this main content section for our About page:

So, we have our two columns, which we created earlier, in which to create the main sections. Let's start with building the left-hand side of the page:

```
<div class="row">
    <div class="col-lg-8">
        <h2>Lorem Ipsum</h2>
        <p>Lorem ipsum dolor sit amet, consectetur adipiscing elit. In
        convallis sapien risus, ut blandit ipsum fringilla a. Donec
        ullamcorper sem non maximus feugiat. Fusce lectus libero,
        blandit id cursus nec, viverra quis nulla. Curabitur nibh ante,
        iaculis eget est a, varius hendrerit nulla. Suspendisse
        blandit, purus nec iaculis semper, eros lorem pharetra lorem,
        tempor blandit velit magna eget ligula. Donec venenatis est
```

```
          luctus elit suscipit facilisis. Proin orci elit, semper id
          mattis in, ullamcorper ac risus. Ut aliquet enim at lorem
          rutrum vulputate. Aenean eu tellus congue, tincidunt sem et,
          molestie enim. Proin luctus lacus consequat dolor posuere
          vulputate.</p>
      </div>
  </div>
```

The preceding code is self-explanatory; we added a heading, h2, and paragraph text. Save it, and let's look at the site now:

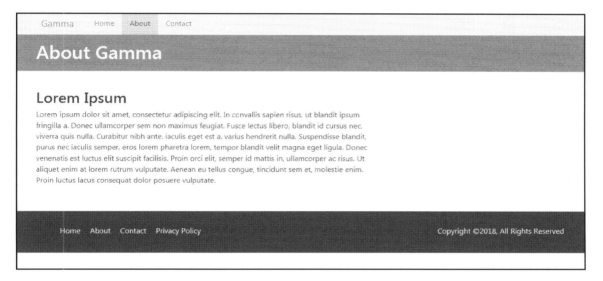

Now, what we're going to do is start working on the accordion section:

```
<div id="accordion" role="tablist">
    <div class="card">
        <div class="card-header" role="tab" id="headingOne">
            <h6 class="mb-0">
              <a data-toggle="collapse" href="#collapseOne" aria-
              expanded="true" aria-controls="collapseOne">
              Collapsible Group Item #1
              </a>
            </h6>
        </div>
    </div>
</div>
```

We are going to add a div with `id="accordion"` and we're going to set the `role` to `tablist`. To create the `accordion` style, we're going to use a card, which is specific to Bootstrap 4. We created a `div` tag with the `card` class and inside it, another `div` tag where we're setting the header. Then, we're going to set our `role` as `tab`, and we'll want to target this, so we're going to give it `id="headingOne"`.

Next, we added a heading, `h6`, and the class is going to be `mb-0`. So, this class is coming out of Bootstrap, and has a bottom margin of 0. Next, we added a link, where we're going to do a `data-toggle`. It's going to be `collapse` so that we have dynamic opening and closing for these sections, and we're going to use `href`—we're just going to say `#collapseOne`. We're going to have our `aria-expanded` set to `true`, and then we add `aria-controls`, which is going to be `collapseOne`. Finally, we're going to give it a title of `Collapsible Group Item #1`.

We are done with the card header now, so let's go ahead and work on the card body:

```
<a id="collapseOne" class="collapse show" role="tabpanel" aria-
labelledby="headingOne" data-parent="#accordion">
    <div class="card-body">
        Anim pariatur cliche reprehenderit, enim eiusmod high life
        accusamus terry richardson ad squid. 3 wolf moon officia aute,
        non cupidatat skateboard dolor brunch. Food truck quinoa
        nesciunt laborum eiusmod. Brunch 3 wolf moon tempor, sunt
        aliqua put a bird on it squid single-origin coffee nulla
        assumenda shoreditch et. Nihil anim keffiyeh helvetica, craft
        beer labore wes anderson cred nesciunt sapiente ea proident. Ad
        vegan excepteur butcher vice lomo. Leggings occaecat craft beer
        farm-to-table, raw denim aesthetic synth nesciunt you probably
        haven't heard of them accusamus labore sustainable VHS.
    </div>
</a>
```

So, here we're going to have a link with an `id="collapseOne"`, so this is what we're targeting from the header. We'll have a `class="collapse show"`, which means that the content of the body will be shown and not hidden. The role will be `tabpanel` and we'll have our `aria-labelledby` containing the `headingOne` ID, and `data-parent` is going to be `#accordion`. Next, we have a `div` tag where we have `card-body` as a class, so we can move from the header into the body, where we can actually just take some text and paste it in.

Make sure that the code for the accordion that we created is inside the large column with span 8. Now, we have to create two more cards inside accordion. Let's copy and paste the card-header and card-body we just created and make two copies of them. There are a few things that have to be updated, which are `id`, `href`, `aria-controls`, and `aria-labelledby`. `collapseOne` will be `collapseTwo` for the second card and `collapseThree` for the third card. Make similar changes to the other features.

Once you have updated the values for both the remaining cards, save them and view the output on the site:

Lorem Ipsum

Lorem ipsum dolor sit amet, consectetur adipiscing elit. In convallis sapien risus, ut blandit ipsum fringilla a. Donec ullamcorper sem non maximus feugiat. Fusce lectus libero, blandit id cursus nec, viverra quis nulla. Curabitur nibh ante, iaculis eget est a, varius hendrerit nulla. Suspendisse blandit, purus nec iaculis semper, eros lorem pharetra lorem, tempor blandit velit magna eget ligula. Donec venenatis est luctus elit suscipit facilisis. Proin orci elit, semper id mattis in, ullamcorper ac risus. Ut aliquet enim at lorem rutrum vulputate. Aenean eu tellus congue, tincidunt sem et, molestie enim. Proin luctus lacus consequat dolor posuere vulputate.

Collapsible Group Item #1

Collapsible Group Item #2

Anim pariatur cliche reprehenderit, enim eiusmod high life accusamus terry richardson ad squid. 3 wolf moon officia aute, non cupidatat skateboard dolor brunch. Food truck quinoa nesciunt laborum eiusmod. Brunch 3 wolf moon tempor, sunt aliqua put a bird on it squid single-origin coffee nulla assumenda shoreditch et. Nihil anim keffiyeh helvetica, craft beer labore wes anderson cred nesciunt sapiente ea proident. Ad vegan excepteur butcher vice lomo. Leggings occaecat craft beer farm-to-table, raw denim aesthetic synth nesciunt you probably haven't heard of them accusamus labore sustainable VHS.

Collapsible Group Item #3

This is what the accordion is going to look like. If you want to have only one part of the body content visible at a time and the other two collapsed, what you have to do is set `class="collapse"` instead of `collapse show`. We will set it to `collapse` for the second and third cards. By clicking on the header, you can collapse or expand the body. Try it out.

Now, we go to our column with span 4, where we have to add an image and some text. We had already created something similar in our `Contact` page. Here is the code:

```
<div class="col-lg-4">
    <img src="img/demo1.jpg" class="demo">
    <h2>Lorem Ipsum</h2>
    <p>Lorem ipsum dolor sit amet, consectetur adipiscing elit. Mauris
      lobortis tempus varius. Sed porttitor ex id lectus interdum
      tristique.</p>
    <a href="#" class="btn btn-outline-secondary" role="button">Read
      More</a>
</div>
```

The code is self-explanatory. Once you save and check this in the browser, you will see something like this:

You will also notice that the `title-bar` name has been changed; you can try that out yourself. In the next section, we're going to do some styling on the `About` page and check out what media queries are.

Styling the About page

We're going to start working on some styling for our `About` page, and in particular the `accordion` that we have. So, what we want to do is add a little bit of margin to that `accordion`. To do this, we're going to target it, and we're going to use `margin-bottom:20px`:

```
#accordion {
    margin-bottom:20px;
}
```

This is a very subtle change; you won't see much difference on the site. Let's go back into our Sass, where we're going to work on our card:

```
.card{
    + .card{margin-top:5px;}
    .card-header {
        h6 {font-weight:normal;}
        a{color:inherit;}
    }
}
```

The card is a class, so we're going to target it with dot. Inside this, we're going to add + to our card, since we're going to use `margin-top`, which is going to be `5px`. The + sign is technically called an adjacent sibling combinator, and because they have the same parent, we put these in a sequence so that one follows immediately after the other. Next, we have to style the `card-header`. `h6` will have `font-weight:normal`, and we're also going to get our hyperlinks, whose color we will `inherit`.

You can see now the header has inherited the same text color, since earlier it was blue. Now, let's go ahead and take a look at our media queries.

Creating custom media breakpoints

Media queries basically help to render content on sites depending on the screen's resolution. Our website is already responsive, so you can go and resize your browser to see the changes take effect. In our case, adding media queries won't make a major difference, but we are going to do a little bit of customization to make it render and look better. Let's go ahead and add media breakpoints, and see how certain content within the website changes its size and layout depending on whether you are viewing the website on a tab, mobile, or desktop:

```
/* media queries */
@media (min-width:1200px) {
    .jumbotron img.showcase-img{
        width:61%;
        margin: 5px 0 0 40px;
    }
}
```

```
@media (min-width:991px) {
    .show-img {
        display:none;
    }
}

@media(min-width: 768px) and (max-width:990px){
    .jumbotron img.app-btn{
        width:30%
    }
    .jumbotron {
        height: 400px !important;
        background-size: 100% 100%
    }
    .jumbotron h1{
        margin-top:10px;
    }
}

@media (max-width:768px){
    .jumbotron {
        height: 350px !important;
        background-size: 100% 100%;
    }
    .jumbotron h1 {
        margin-top: 10px;
    }
}

@media (max-width:500px){
    .jumbotron {
        height: 450px !important;
        background-image: none;
        text-align: center;
    }
    .jumbotron img.app-btn {
        width: 60%;
        margin: 0 auto 30px auto;
        display: block;
    }
    section#feature ul li {
        font-size: 19px !important;
    }
    footer p {
        float: none;
        text-align: center;
        padding-top: 20px;
```

```
        }
    }
```

In the preceding code, you can see that we have used min-width and max-width. These widths are basically the breakpoints that we add, depending on the device. We have targeted devices of all sizes in the preceding code and customized the content on the page as per the resolution. We have reduced the size of the jumbotron image, added padding and margins, and more.

When we say min-width is 768px, it means devices that are greater than or equal to 768px. If max-width is set to 768px, it is targeting devices that are less than or equal to 768px.

Save the preceding code, and check the output on the website. If you go ahead and shrink your browser, you will see the content adapting to the resolution. You will see the jumbotron image reducing in size as it hits the different breakpoints. Try it out; you should see something similar to the following screenshot:

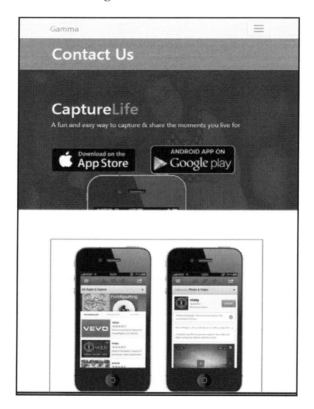

This should complete the layouts that we want for this website. What we're going to do next is take a look at the grid settings in isolation to really understand what's going on with the way we've chosen some of the values. We want to understand what that means and how it works. One last thing we have to do on the site is install Font Awesome.

Installing Font Awesome

In this section, we're going be installing Font Awesome for our website. This is going to require a change to our `gulpfile` so that it can be used as part of our base template. So, instead of the template that we had, we're just going to enhance it and we're going to have the template that includes Font Awesome as well. You can go to the Font Awesome website at `https://fontawesome.com/?from=io` and download it:

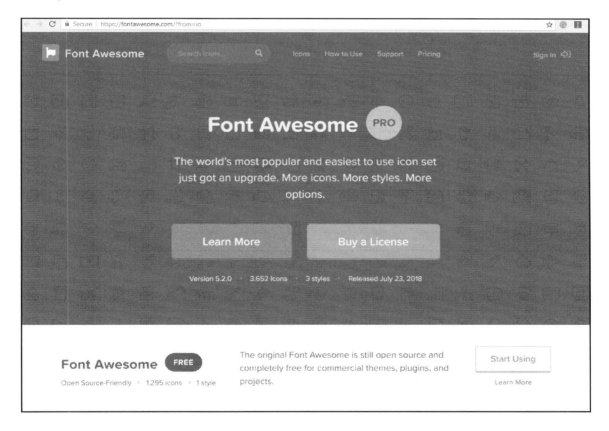

However, we're actually going to go through npm and install Font Awesome. Then, we're going to see how to make the modifications in the `gulpfile` and add the local reference into our HTML files, just like we've done with Bootstrap and jQuery as well. So, let's go ahead and go into Visual Studio Code, where we're going to do the installation of Font Awesome. Alright, so on the command line, we will type the command:

```
npm install font-awesome
```

Which is going to download Font Awesome and add it into our `node_modules`:

```
C:\Users\leenapatil\Desktop\Code\P1>npm install font-awesome
npm WARN test1@1.0.0 No description
npm WARN test1@1.0.0 No repository field.

+ font-awesome@4.7.0
updated 1 package in 31.096s
```

If you go and check inside `node_modules`, you will see `font-awesome` in the list. If not, click on the Refresh button and it will appear:

```
⊿ font-awesome
  ▷ css
  ⊿ fonts
      fontawesome-webfont.eot
      fontawesome-webfont.svg
      fontawesome-webfont.ttf
      fontawesome-webfont.woff
      fontawesome-webfont.woff2
      FontAwesome.otf
  ▷ less
  ▷ scss
    .npmignore
    HELP-US-OUT.txt
  {} package.json
```

As you can see, we have a number of fonts, and we want to move all of these into our local location. So, let's go to our `src` folder and add a `fonts` folder. Okay, so in our `gulpfile`, we're going to put a new task right here, just below `move-js`, so we're going to start this off like the others with the `gulp.task`:

```
gulp.task('move-fonts', function() {
    return gulp.src(['node_modules/font-awesome/fonts/*'])
    .pipe(gulp.dest('src/fonts'))
    .pipe(browserSync.stream())
})
```

Let's call this task `move-fonts`. Here, we're going to follow the same pattern: we will have a function, and it will have three lines of code inside, so it's not going to be quite as big as some of the others because the paths aren't quite as involved. So, first, we're going to return `gulp.src`, and in here we're going to have an array, which is going to go into `node_modules/font-awesome/fonts/*`. We are using a `*` because we're going to take all of those and move them. That completes that part. Now, for the chaining on these pipes that we have, we're going to do a `gulp.dest`, which goes in `src/fonts`, and we're going to do one more pipe, which is going to be a `browserSync.stream`. So, we'll save that and now we need to do a few other modifications. Alright, so we have to also add a path in our `gulp.watch`:

```
gulp.watch(['node_modules/bootstrap/scss/bootstrap.scss','node_modules/font
-awesome/scss/font-awesome.scss', 'src/scss/*.scss'],['compile-sass'])
gulp.watch("src/*.html").on('change', browserSync.reload)
```

We are going to update the first `watch`. So, right after this Bootstrap, we're going to go ahead and use `node_modules/font-awesome/scss/font-awesome.scss` within single quotes. That should be all we need in that modification. Now, we have the `move-fonts` task created earlier, which isn't integrated yet, so it needs to be triggered. To do that, we will add it after `move-js`, as shown in the following code:

```
gulp.task('default', ['move-js','move-fonts', 'launch-server'])
```

Save it, and go ahead and run `gulp` on our integrated terminal, making sure that everything is going to run in this new task. If we go and check our `fonts` folder under the `src` directory, you will see that all of the fonts have been imported. Go back into VS Code, where we're going to open this up and see that we have all of our fonts in there:

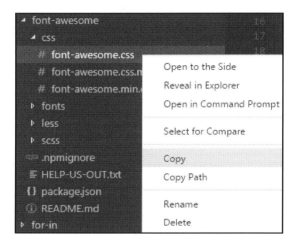

Now, we need to make the modifications inside of our HTML files. We have to add our `font-awesome` CSS file as follows:

```
<link rel="stylesheet" href="/css/font-awesome.css">
<!-- Bootstrap CSS -->
<link rel="stylesheet" href="/css/bootstrap.css">
<link rel="stylesheet" href="/css/style.css">
</head>
```

Instead of creating a whole task just for this one file, we can just move that CSS because we're not working with the CSS file for Font Awesome, and we're not really concerned about having to move it every time we use it. We are going move it this one time, and it's going to be there:

For this, we will go to `font-awesome`, and under the `css` folder we will right-click and copy `font-awesome.css`, then paste it into the `css` folder inside our `src` directory, as shown in the following screenshot:

We have two other files, `about.html` and `contact.html`, where we have to paste the following line of code, like we did earlier:

```
<link rel="stylesheet" href="/css/font-awesome.css">
```

Now, we can go back to the browser and check that everything's working. We can see that it's not really causing any errors. What I want to do is just inspect and make sure that we don't have any errors:

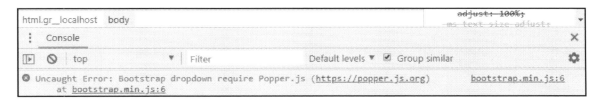

It says that the Bootstrap drop-down requires `Popper.js`. We can go ahead and add that `Popper` reference, but it looks like Font Awesome is working fine. `Popper` will go at the bottom of our `index` file and make the following update:

```
<!-- jQuery first, then Popper.js, then Bootstrap JS -->
<script src="/js/jquery.min.js" ></script>
<script src="/js/popper.min.js" ></script>
<script src="/js/tether.min.js" ></script>
<script src="/js/bootstrap.min.js" ></script>
</body>
</html>
```

Once you save and run `gulp` on the terminal, the site should work fine. Okay, so that completes our `Popper` implementation as well.

We are done implementing font awesome and `Popper.js`. Now, we will go ahead and understand the grid systems.

Grid analysis

We're going to go through a little bit more in-depth analysis on the grid layouts, so let's go to the `https://getbootstrap.com/` website and under **Documentation**, click on **Layout** and then click **Grid**. If you scroll down, you will see some of the configurations that are allowed with the grid. Here they are:

	Extra small <576px	Small ≥576px	Medium ≥768px	Large ≥992px	Extra large ≥1200px
Max container width	None (auto)	540px	720px	960px	1140px
Class prefix	`.col-`	`.col-sm-`	`.col-md-`	`.col-lg-`	`.col-xl-`
# of columns	12				
Gutter width	30px (15px on each side of a column)				
Nestable	Yes				
Column ordering	Yes				

As you can see, we have different class prefixes for different sizes. What we're going to do now is actually go to a playground where we can use these configurations and see what impact they have. Let's search for w3 schools **Bootstrap 4 Grid System** in Google, and go to the link `https://www.w3schools.com/bootstrap4/bootstrap_grid_system.asp`. Scroll down to the *Basic Structure of a Bootstrap 4 Grid* section and click on the **Try it Yourself** button to access the playground:

Basic Structure of a Bootstrap 4 Grid

The following is a basic structure of a Bootstrap 4 grid:

```
<!-- Control the column width, and how they should appear on different devices -->
<div class="row">
  <div class="col-*-*"></div>
  <div class="col-*-*"></div>
  <div class="col-*-*"></div>
</div>

<!-- Or let Bootstrap automatically handle the layout -->
<div class="row">
  <div class="col"></div>
  <div class="col"></div>
  <div class="col"></div>
  <div class="col"></div>
</div>
```

Try it Yourself »

Let's remove all of the extra lines of code and only keep the ones shown in the following screenshot. We have replaced the percentage with `some text`:

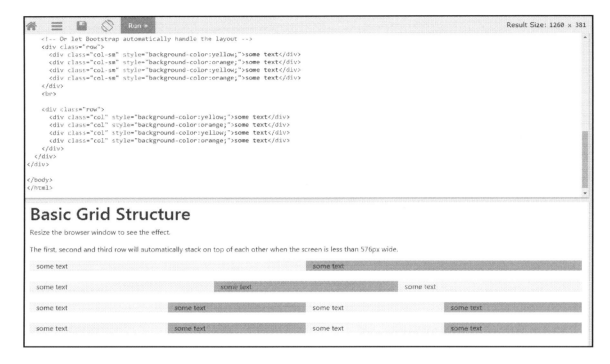

The first two columns have a span of 12 each, which would add up to 24, and the next two columns have a spans of 3 and 9, respectively, which would add up to 12. The maximum span is 12 for Bootstrap – you can't exceed that. Hence, the first two columns are stacked one below the other, whereas the next two columns fit perfectly on the screen. Let's see what happens when we resize the browser:

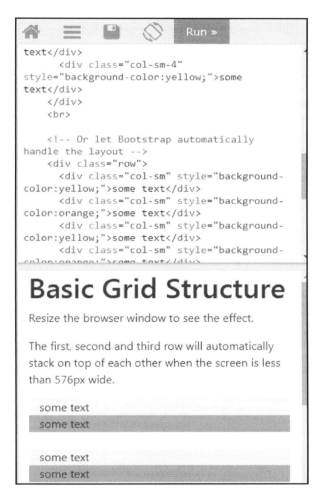

You can see that when we shrink the browser, the first two columns remain as they are, whereas the other two columns have changed. This was for a small-screen device. Now, we will look at a medium-screen device with columns that sum up to more than 12 and exactly 12:

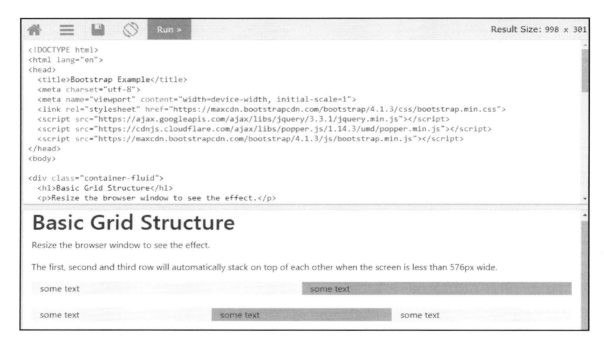

As you can see in the preceding screenshot, since the columns with a span 7 each sum up to 14, we have them stacked one below the other, whereas the next two columns seem to fit the screen perfectly. Let's resize the browser to see the effects:

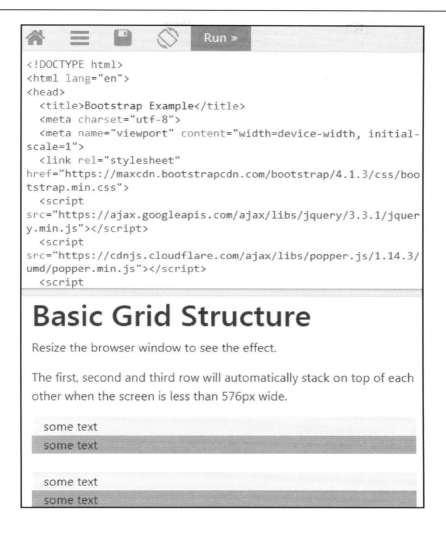

As you can see, when the size of the screen is smaller, the columns stack one below the other. You can try it out for different spans and see how the browser reacts. This is basically how a grid system works.

Summary

In this chapter, we covered a lot of things while building the photosharing website project. The first thing we did was focus on just building the website layout, and that included our menu, the jumbotron, and creating those main content sections. As we built these, we went out, saw the effect it had on the website, went back, did a few more changes to the code, and then checked the website to see what impact anything we were doing was having visually on the website. We created a few variables that we could make use of in our Sass SCSS file, along with some CSS styling in the same file, and then when our Gulp task runs, it compiles that Sass down into a `.css` file, which of course the website can then use.

We added in our `Contact` page and our `About` page, and then we got into some custom media breakpoints and saw some different areas that we would want to adjust, depending on how we want the website to look at that particular breakpoint. Then, we installed Font Awesome using `npm`. We also did grid analysis to understand the impact of different columns and, let's say, the overuse of a column.

In the next chapter, we are going to create a resume website, which is another pretty interesting website, and we're actually going to adhere to the limit of 12. Now that we've explored the impact of these differences here, we're just going to stick with the conventional methods used inside of Bootstrap on the column's max width.

4
Building a Resume Website

In this chapter, we are going to build a responsive resume website. We will be adding different sections to our resume in this chapter, and the grid system will play an important role. We will have sections such as about me, contact information, education, experience, skills, services, and recent projects that you might have done.

We will be covering the following topics:

- Revising the `gulpfile`
- Creating the HTML layout
- Styling the `Home` page
- Adding the education and skills section
- Adding the services and projects section

Revising the gulpfile

The first thing we need to do is bring the templates we created earlier into this project. Let's open the gulpfile, where we're going to make a few efficiency changes to help us with a few different things in this project. Here is what the folder structure and gulpfile look like:

What we've done is taken template 1, then taken those files, including the node_modules, and put them into the P2 folder. This is going to be our template 2, and is the template that we want be using going forward. Make sure that whenever you're taking node_modules, dropping them in, and using a package.json that's already there, you want to perform npm install in the terminal so that you can be sure that all of those packages that are related to the package.json are installed. Now, let's go ahead and check out the package.json file:

```
{
  "name": "test1",
  "version": "1.0.0",
  "description": "",
  "main": "index.js",
  "scripts": {
```

```
"test": "echo \"Error: no test specified\" && exit 1"
},
"author": "",
"license": "ISC",
"devDependencies": {
"bootstrap": "^4.0.0-beta",
"browser-sync": "^2.18.13",
"font-awesome": "^4.7.0",
"gulp": "^3.9.1",
"gulp-sass": "^3.1.0",
"jquery": "^3.2.1",
"tether": "^1.4.0"
}
}
```

This `package.json` file is going to be template 2; it has jQuery, tether, and Font Awesome. All of these should be installed if you don't have them in your `node_modules` that you're carrying over from template 1, for example, or maybe from somewhere else.

In our current gulpfile, we are not moving `font-awesome.css` from `node_modules` to `src`. In our last project, we manually moved it to our `src/css` folder. This time, we are going to have Gulp actually populate the file.

For our jQuery, everything is looking pretty good, except for Popper, but that's another unique case because of the versioning going on: Popper versus the beta of Bootstrap 4. Once the final version Bootstrap is out, Popper should be able to get populated through the `gulpfile` by doing an `npm install` of that Popper. We saw previously that this doesn't work right now. So, what we're going to do with Gulp is mainly move the CSS and `font-awesome.css` file. We're going to have it do the move for us, and then later on when Popper is more compatible through `npm` you can just add another path.

Since we're just moving files to a new location, we will have to create a new task as follows:

```
gulp.task('move-css', function() {
    return gulp.src(['node_modules/font-awesome/css/font-
    awesome.css'])
    .pipe(gulp.dest('src/css'))
    .pipe(browserSync.stream())
})
```

The code is self-explanatory; we are basically moving the `font-awesome.css` file and dropping it inside the `src/css` path. This change is also going to be a part of our template 2, which we are going to use moving forward.

To execute this task, we have to add the task name now. Let's add that:

```
//run gulp
//launch server and browser
//execute js task
gulp.task('default', ['move-js','move-fonts','move-css', 'launch-server'])
```

We're not watching this file, so it's not going to run. What we can do instead is run `gulp` in the terminal. Now, we can see that `font-awesome` has been added to the `css` folder:

We have one more thing left to do: we have to go to the `index.html` file and paste the reference that we used from our first project to Font Awesome:

```
<!-- Bootstrap CSS -->
<link rel="stylesheet" href="css/font-awesome.css">
<link rel="stylesheet" href="/css/bootstrap.css">
<link rel="stylesheet" href="/css/style.css">
```

Alright, so this is going to be the template that we are going to use moving forward. What we're going to do next is jump into creating our `index.html`. We're also going to be working inside of our Sass file.

Creating the HTML layout

Now, we're going to get into creating our layout for our resume website. Here, we're going to have two columns, as you can see in the target site shown in the following screenshot. We're going to have our footer, our header at the top stretching across, and our picture as well:

Now, we're going to look at our `index.html`. To start off, we will first remove our `Hello, world!` and also remove the styling from our `style.scss` file, if any. Before we start working on our resume website, let's add the `popper.min.js` script as follows:

```
<!-- Optional JavaScript -->
<!-- jQuery first, then Popper.js, then Bootstrap JS -->
<script src="/js/jquery.min.js"></script>
<script src="/js/tether.min.js"></script>
<script src="/js/popper.min.js"></script>
<script src="/js/bootstrap.min.js"></script>
```

Now, in our `index.html` file, we're going to start off with a container, which is going to be inside a `div`:

```
<div class="container main-container">
<img src="img/person.png" class="profile-img">
<header>
  <h1>HELLO, <br>my name is <strong>John Doe</strong> and I am a web
  developer</h1>
</header>
<img src="img/line.png" class="line">
</div>
```

As you can see in the preceding code, this is going to be our main `div`, which means that we have a `container` class, and we're going to have one more class called `main-container`. Now, this is not a Bootstrap 4 class; this is something that we're creating that will help us with our styling. So, next, we're going to have the image of a person, which is present in the `img` folder. The image we're going to use is `person.png`. We will have a class for that as well, `profile-img`. Next, we're going to start with a header tag and in here we're going to introduce **John Doe** (or you can introduce yourself with a sentence) and save it. Now, we're going to continue building so that we have our header, and then we're going to have a line that divides, so we're going to add an image called `line.png` and we'll have a `class="line"`. Let's save this and go and check out our browser:

HELLO,
my name is John Doe and I am a web developer

Here, we can see our profile picture, a sentence introducing the profile, and also the line. We're missing a lot of formatting, but this is the beginning of it. The classes we created are going to help us with some adjusting of the positioning of these elements.

Now, we're going to get into our columns. We're going to start with a `div class="row"` and we're going to use 7 and 5 because that's going to equal 12. In this project, and going forward, we're not going to make any columns where the column count adds up to over 12 like we did in the last one. We have already seen the effects of doing that: it will just stack them, and you'll get columns that span all the way across when you exceed 12, which is we're going to adhere to the Bootstrap 4 recommendations of staying under a total count of 12. So, because we only have two columns, we're going to make use of 7 and 5:

```
<div class="row">
  <div class="col-md-7">
    <h2># About Me</h2>
    <p>Lorem ipsum dolor sit amet, consectetur adipiscing elit. Ut
    aliquet mi ornare massa gravida, auctor accumsan ipsum rhoncus.
    Vestibulum in erat tempor, rutrum diam fringilla, feugiat augue.
    Morbi dapibus bibendum erat, nec euismod lacus ultrices eu. Aliquam
    a bibendum ante, id convallis massa. Aliquam iaculis</p>
  </div>
  <div class="col-md-5">
    <h2># Contact Info</h2>
    <ul class="contact-list">
      <li><img src="img/phone.png"> (978) 555-5555</li>
      <li><img src="img/email.png"> johndoe@gmail.com</li>
      <li><img src="img/facebook.png"> Facebook
      <span>facebook.com/johndoe</span></li>
      <li><img src="img/twitter.png"> Twitter
      <span>twitter.com/johndoe</span></li>
    </ul>
  </div>
</div>
```

We're going to go with `col-md-7` and `col-md-5` here. We will start by populating the first column. We will add a heading, h2, which is going to be `# About Me`, and after that we're going to have a paragraph with some Lorem Ipsum, which you can copy and paste in. Now, let's move on to our second column. Here, we will also have a heading, h2, which is going to be `# Contact Info`. Now, below Contact Info, we're actually going to have an unordered list. So, we're going to start with ul, whose class is `contact-list`, and next we're going to reference our images for the list. We'll have our text content as well.

Here, we are going to add the source of the `src="img/phone.png"` image. Similarly, we will add a picture for email, Facebook, and Twitter. We will then add the respective details, as shown in the previous code. We're going to have a link as well so that inside of the `span` tag, we have added the Facebook and Twitter links. Let's save and check out what our browser looks like:

Here, you can see the dramatic difference, without doing any kind of styling, when compared to our target site shown at the start of this section. In the next section, we're going to start applying the styling that gives coloring, spacing, and bold. We have a few classes that we've already created, `contact-list`, `main-container`, `profile-img`, and `line`. These are going to go inside of our `style.scss`.

Styling the home page

In this section, we are going to add style to our home page. Before we get into our styling, we want to go ahead and create four variables in our `style.scss` file:

```
$primary-color:#3b5a76;
$background-color:#ededed;
$text-color:#363636;
$font:16px;
```

So, here we have added a primary color, background color, text color, and font size. Now, we're going to start off with a body tag in our `style.scss` file:

```
body {
    padding-bottom:0;
    font-family: 'Open Sans', Arial, Tahoma;
    color:$text-color;
    background: $background-color;
    font-size: $font;
}
```

For the body, we will have no padding on the bottom; we're going to reference particular fonts that are being used, so we'll have `Open Sans`. This is inside of single quotes because it is a compound word. We'll have `Arial` and `Tahoma` as well. Next, we added color, which is going to be our `$text-color`variable. We then added a background and assigned the `$background-color` variable, and finally assigned the `$font` variable to `font-size`. Save these changes. Now, we will run `gulp` and check out what the changes look like on our browser:

We can see some differences here. We can see that the font is a little more slender than what we had before; it's also not completely black. The background has got some gray to it. Let's move ahead with styling our other tags. We will first work on the h2 tags, making them all caps and adding color to them, as we saw in our target site:

```
h2 {
    font-weight:700;
    text-transform: uppercase;
    line-height: 1.4em;
    font-size: 1.5em;
    margin-top:20px;
}
```

So, we have added a font-weight of 700, which is basically for thickening the fonts, and then we added text-transform to make our text uppercase, so we're not having to type that uppercase in; we're just going to do it through styling. We're going to adjust the line height, which is going to be 1.4em, and we're going to also change font size of h2 to 1.5em. Then, we're going to add a margin to the top, which is going to be 20px. The values that we are adding to font-size and line-height depend on how you want it to appear visually. You can save, run gulp, and check the browser for changes. To see how these styles are affecting the browser, you can always right-click and **Inspect element**.

Now, we're going to do our coloring. Here is the code for this:

```
.primary,
strong,
h2 {
    color: $primary-color;
}
```

We have our primary class coming in, along with strong and h2. We will give it a color of $primary-color and then save it. So, the color is going to affect the headings with h2 tags, and the text that is within the strong tags, such as John Doe in our case. We don't have a primary class at this point – that's coming down the road. Let's go back and continue building out our page.

We have our main-container that we're going to work on now, which is a class:

```
.main-container {
    background: #fff;
    position:relative;
    top:80px;
    margin-bottom:80px;
    padding:0 30px 30px 30px;
}
```

We have kept the background white, the position relative, and the top property to `80px`. We have also added a `margin-bottom` and padding. Let's save it and check the changes in our browser:

Right-click and **Inspect** `main-container`. You can see the background changes and how the top and margin properties are affecting the layout. You can check out the difference by checking or unchecking the properties on the right-hand side of your **Inspect element** panel, as shown in the preceding screenshot.

Okay, so continuing with building out parts of our resume page, we also made use of a `header` tag, so we are going to start with that:

```
header {
    min-height: 100px;
    overflow: auto;
}
```

So, we have a `header` tag where we have set the minimum height to `100px` and we're going to have our overflow, which is going to be set to `auto`. If you save and check the website now for the changes, they are going to be very subtle. The `min-height` is basically going to push the line down a bit and overflow is set to auto so that if the text flows out of div, it will automatically wrap the text. In our case, that is not a concern, but to be on the safe side, we have added this CSS property.

Next, we are going to work on the `h1` tag, which contains our text. We already added styling on the header, so now we're going to look at some styling on this `h1` while we are here. This is going to be just for the header:

```
header h1 {
    margin: 0;
    padding: 20px 0 0 0;
    font-size: 2.2em;
    font-weight: 700;
    text-transform: uppercase;
    letter-spacing: -1px;
    text-align: center;
    line-height: 1.4em;
}
```

Inside of the header, we're going to reference the `h1` as a tags, not as class, and we're going to tighten it up with no margin. Next, we're going to have padding on top so that we can have a little separation from the picture. We're going to do a little bit of adjusting of the font size. Again, this is a preference; just choose what you want your font to look like. So, we're overriding what is happening with the default font that we have, and we're going to set our `font-weight` to `700` as well. If you check the target site, you will see that the text below the profile image should be uppercase, which is currently not the case, except for **HELLO**. So, everything inside of `h1`, which is everything we saw at the top of the page, we're going to make uppercase by setting `text-transform` to `uppercase`, and then we're going to have `letter-spacing`, which is going to be `-1px`. Here, we're pulling the text in. Next, we center align our text. Finally, we're going to use a common line height, `1.4em`, and save it. Now, if we run `gulp` and see our page in the browser, you will see something like the following:

As you can see, we can see the changes that have taken place. We can see our CSS properties on the right hand side of our **Elements** panel. I have unchecked letter-spacing in the preceding screenshot to show you the difference, since you can see that there is spacing between letters. You can try it out yourself.

The most important thing to remember is that all of your styling should happen in the `style.scss` file and not the `.css` file.

Now, we have few more classes such as `profile-img`, `line`, **and** `contact-list` where we have to apply styles. We will start also building the main content for our website.

Adding the education and skills section

Now, we're going to start building upon the rest of our resume page. We're going to add the footer first because there's not much to it, and then we're going to begin building out the content for the About Me and Contact pages. The following screenshot explains what we are planning to build:

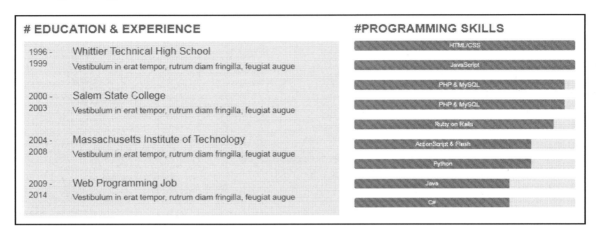

On the left, we have education and experience, along with the relevant years, and on the right we have progress bars indicating how much of the skill is available. So, let's go ahead and get into our code editor. As mentioned previously, we're going to add the footer now. We are going to add that right above the script files, which is going to be a semantic tag, and we're not going to have any classes inside of it:

```
<footer>
  <div class="container">
     <P>Copyright &copy;2018, All Rights Reserved</P>
  </div>
</footer>
```

Inside the `footer`, we have a `div` tag with a `container` class, and then we added a paragraph for our copyright message. Alright, so that is our footer, which we'll come back to later in order to style it. Now, we're going to move on to creating some of the other sections that we talked about earlier.

We are going to create two columns as we did for the About Me and Contact pages. The first column will have a span of 7 and second column will have a span of 5. Let's start with the first column:

```
<div class="row">
    <div class="col-md-7">
      <h2># Education & Experience</h2>
      <div class="media">
        <div class="media-left">
          1996 - 1999
        </div>
        <div class="media-body">
          <h5 class="media-heading">Whittier Technical High School</h5>
          <p>Vestibulum in erat tempor, rutrum diam fringilla, feugiat
            augue</p>
        </div>
    </div>
</div>
```

What we're going to add is a heading, h2, and then we put our title, # Education & Experience, inside it. Now, we're getting into some text, and as you can see, the details are inside a gray box. To create that effect, we're going to use a media class, and media is going to be one of our custom classes that doesn't come from Bootstrap 4. We're going to start adding a few more custom classes, which we will use later on to style the sections. Now, we have added another one, media-left, where we'll have our dates. Next, we're going to have another div and another class, which we're going to call media-body. This is how we're breaking the content horizontally into columns. We're going to add a heading, h5, on this one, which has another class="media-heading", and we will add the school name, Whittier Technical High School. Then, we will add a paragraph, which will have some Lorem Ipsum inside it. Basically, media-left is going to push the dates to the left and, in a similar fashion, details of education and experience will be pushed to the right by its class.

We have only added one entry to our education and experience section, so there's three more to go.

The code for the years 2000-2003 is as follows:

```
<div class="media">
    <div class="media-left">
    2000 - 2003
    </div>
    <div class="media-body">
      <h5 class="media-heading">Salem State College</h5>
      <p>Vestibulum in erat tempor, rutrum diam fringilla, feugiat
```

```
      augue</p>
    </div>
  </div>
```

The code for the years 2004-2008 is as follows:

```
<div class="media">
    <div class="media-left">
      2004 - 2008
    </div>
    <div class="media-body">
      <h5 class="media-heading">Massachusetts Institute of
      Technology</h5>
      <p>Vestibulum in erat tempor, rutrum diam fringilla, feugiat
      augue</p>
    </div>
</div>
```

The code for the years 2009-2014 is as follows:

```
<div class="media">
    <div class="media-left">
      2009 - 2014
    </div>
    <div class="media-body">
      <h5 class="media-heading">Web Programming Job</h5>
      <p>Vestibulum in erat tempor, rutrum diam fringilla, feugiat
      augue</p>
    </div>
</div>
```

Now, we are getting into the other side, which is Programming Skills. Here is the code for this:

```
<div class="col-md-5">
  <h2>#Programming Skills</h2>
    <div class="progress">
      <div class="progress-bar progress-bar-striped"
       role="progressbar" aria-valuenow="0" aria-valuemin="0" aria-
       valuemax="100" style="min-width:2em;width:100%">
       HTML/CSS
    </div>
</div>
```

So, again, we're going to go ahead with an h2 for our header. We have a div with a class called progress, and then we add another div where we are going to add two more classes, progress-bar and progress-bar-striped. These two classes come from Bootstrap 4. We will throw a role in there for progressbar; aria is going to be a valuenow of 0. So, these parts of the aria controls are here to tell you how much of the progress is actually being used because it's a graphic, so visually you can see it there. Then, we're going to have valuemin and valuemax set to 0 and 100, respectively. Finally, we have added our inline styles. The reason we have inline styles is to specify the width. Each programming skill will have a different width, so in this case, we have set it to 100%. We then added the programming skill HTML/CSS.

Now, we will be adding our other programming skills in a similar fashion. We will be copying the code within the progress class and updating the width and the programming languages. The code for JavaScript is as follows:

```
<div class="progress">
    <div class="progress-bar progress-bar-striped" role="progressbar"
    aria-valuenow="0" aria-valuemin="0" aria-valuemax="100"
    style="min-width:2em;width:100%">JavaScript
    </div>
</div>
```

The code for PHP and MySQL is as follows:

```
 <div class="progress">
     <div class="progress-bar progress-bar-striped" role="progressbar"
     aria-valuenow="0" aria-valuemin="0" aria-valuemax="100"
     style="min-width:2em;width:95%">
     PHP & MySQL
     </div>
 </div>
```

The code for Ruby on Rails is as follows:

```
<div class="progress">
    <div class="progress-bar progress-bar-striped" role="progressbar"
    aria-valuenow="0" aria-valuemin="0" aria-valuemax="100" style="min-
    width:2em;width:90%">
    Ruby on Rails
    </div>
</div>
```

The code for `ActionScrip` and `Flash` is as follows:

```
<div class="progress">
    <div class="progress-bar progress-bar-striped" role="progressbar"
    aria-valuenow="0" aria-valuemin="0" aria-valuemax="100" style="min-
    width:2em;width:80%">
    ActionScript & Flash
    </div>
</div>
```

The code for `Python` is as follows:

```
<div class="progress">
    <div class="progress-bar progress-bar-striped" role="progressbar"
    aria-valuenow="0" aria-valuemin="0" aria-valuemax="100" style="min-
    width:2em;width:80%">
    Python
    </div>
</div>
```

The code for `Java` is as follows:

```
<div class="progress">
    <div class="progress-bar progress-bar-striped" role="progressbar"
    aria-valuenow="0" aria-valuemin="0" aria-valuemax="100" style="min-
    width:2em;width:70%">
    Java
    </div>
</div>
```

The code for `C#` is as follows:

```
<div class="progress">
    <div class="progress-bar progress-bar-striped" role="progressbar"
    aria-valuenow="0" aria-valuemin="0" aria-valuemax="100"
    style="min-width:2em;width:70%">
    C#
    </div>
</div>
```

Let's save it and check the output on the browser:

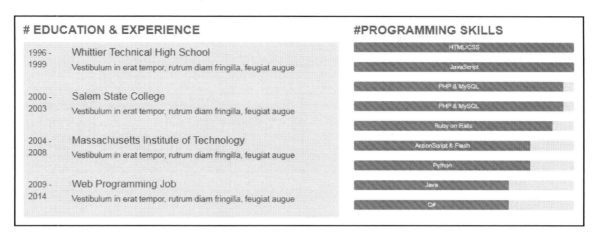

Now that we are done adding the content, let's go ahead and start adding styles to these.

Adding styles to the education and skills section

Our content for the resume page has been added, so let's go to our `style.scss` file and start adding styles to them. We will first target a few of our classes. In the following code, we have added styles to `row`, `profile-img`, `line`, and `contact-list`:

```
.row {
    margin-bottom:20px;
}
.profile-img {
    width:160px;
    display:block;
    margin: 0 auto -80px;
    position:relative;
    top:-80px;
}
.line {
    max-width: 100%;
}
.contact-list{
    padding:0;
    margin:0;
}
```

To find out what each of these CSS properties does, go to the browser, right-click, and **Inspect element**. As we did earlier, in the **Elements** panel, you can check and uncheck each of the CSS properties shown on the right-hand side to see its effect on the page.

There are a couple more things related to `contact-list` that we have to fix. One is `contact-list li`, and the other is `contact-list span`. Here is the CSS code:

```
.contact-list li {
    list-style:none;
    font-weight:bold;
    line-height: 3.2rem;
}

.contact-list span {
    display:block;
    margin:0;
    padding:0;
    line-height: 0.1rem;
    margin-left: 37px;
    font-size: 15px;
    color: #ccc;
}
```

Let's save the file and go and look at the browser now:

Now, everything looks as expected after we added the styles. Let's move ahead and work on our media and media-left classes:

```
.media {
    background:$background-color;
    padding:10px;
}

.media-left {
    width:85px;
    padding:0 10px 0 0;
}
```

Now, we are left with the progress class. Let's go ahead and add CSS properties to it:

```
.progress {
    height:1.25rem;
    margin-bottom:1.25rem;
}
```

Let's look at what the page looks like on the browser:

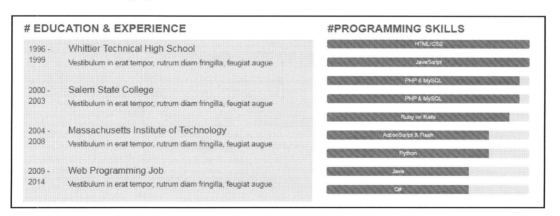

It came out as we planned. Now, let's just do our footer real quick. Here is the CSS code for that:

```
footer {
    background: $primary-color;
    color:#fff;
    text-align: center;
    padding-top:20px;
    padding-bottom: 20px;
}
```

Now, our footer is also ready. This is what it looks like:

The only thing left to do is add the services and projects to our resume page, which we will see in the next section.

Adding services and projects

Now, we're getting to the tail end of this project. Before we go ahead and start building our services and projects, we will get a glimpse of what we are working toward. Here is the last section that we are building for our resume page:

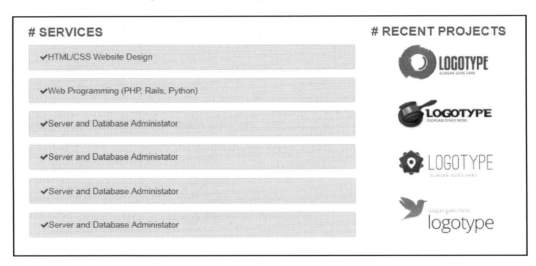

As we did earlier, we are again going to have a row with two columns: one with class="col-md-7" and another with class="col-md-5". Let's start populating our first column:

```
<div class="col-md-7">
  <h2># Services</h2>
  <div class="alert alert-success" role="alert">
    <i class="fa fa-check" aria-hidden="true"></i>HTML/CSS Website
    Design
    </div>
```

```
    <div class="alert alert-info" role="alert">
       <i class="fa fa-check" aria-hidden="true"></i>Web Programming
       (PHP, Rails, Python)
    </div>
    <div class="alert alert-success" role="alert">
      <i class="fa fa-check" aria-hidden="true"></i>Server and
      Database Administator
    </div>
    <div class="alert alert-info" role="alert">
      <i class="fa fa-check" aria-hidden="true"></i>Server and
      Database Administator
    </div>
    <div class="alert alert-success" role="alert">
      <i class="fa fa-check" aria-hidden="true"></i>Server and
      Database Administator
    </div>
    <div class="alert alert-info" role="alert">
      <i class="fa fa-check" aria-hidden="true"></i>Server and
      Database Administator
    </div>
  </div>
</div>
```

Alright, we start the column by adding the h2 header and calling it `# Services`. Next, we have added a `div` tag where we have our `alert` and `alert-success` classes. These two classes come from Bootstrap. This will help us get the colors under the `Services` section, as shown in the earlier target screenshot. We're going to add a `role="alert"` next. Inside that, we're going to have an italics tag, which is going to have the Font Awesome classes `fa` and `fa-check`, and then we have our `aria-hidden="true"`, followed by our title, `HTML/CSS Website Design`, and finally we close our `div`. So, the next step is pretty straightforward: you have to make five more copies of the `div` tag we just created and update the necessary areas, as shown previously in the code. To get the blue and green colors in an alternate order, we will have to replace `alert-success` with `alert-info`. Make sure you update the title as well.

Now, we are going to move on to our next column. This part is going to be pretty quick. Here is the code:

```
<div class="col-md-5">
    <h2># Recent Projects</h2>
    <ul class="work-list">
      <li><a href="#"><img src="img/work1.png"></a></li>
      <li><a href="#"><img src="img/work2.png"></a></li>
      <li><a href="#"><img src="img/work3.png"></a></li>
      <li><a href="#"><img src="img/work4.png"></a></li>
    </ul>
</div>
```

What we have done here is add a header h2 and give the title as # Recent Projects. Next comes our custom class work list. We're creating this class for these different unordered lists because they don't all follow the same visuals, so it gives us control over particular ones. Alright, so we're going to mock out an actual link and we're going to use images, so we have img src="img/work1.png". There's three more of these, so we will copy and paste the code. Make sure the image file names are updated to work2.png, work3.png, and work4.png, respectively. Now, let's go back to our style.scss file and add styles to our work-list class. Here is the CSS code:

```
.work-list li {
    list-style: none;
    float: left;
    padding: 0 10px 0 10px;
    margin-bottom: 30px;
}
```

Now, save the file, run it, and let's see it in the browser:

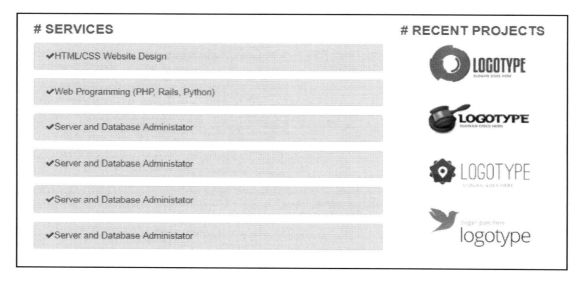

There we are! We can see that our logos are aligned, and everything here is looking good. Finally, our **SERVICES** and **RECENT PROJECTS** section is also ready. We have now created a great-looking resume site that is also responsive.

Summary

In this chapter, we created a resume site that is fully responsive. We created several rows and columns to accomplish this. We did a number of transformations on our fonts, including some colors, as well as some uppercasing. We saw progress bars that looked like images but were created using Bootstrap components. We also used a gulpfile to move `font-awesome.css`, and then we added that into our main task so that we didn't have to worry about moving that file manually. It was a good enhancement to our gulpfile. With this, we have completed our resume website build, and in the next chapter we are going to build a social network frontend.

5
Social Network Frontend

In this chapter, we are going to be creating the frontend of a social media website. Like other sites, it's focused on layout rather than integrating a lot of functionalities. We are going to target the following site to build our social media website:

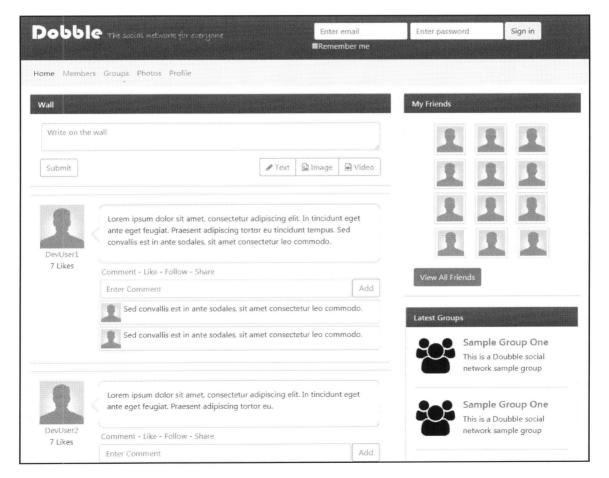

So, there are some new things that we're going to be introduced to in this project. As you can see on the wall section, we're going to be using cards. There's a hierarchy to building cards, similar to a button or a navigation where with the root of nav or navbar, you then start expanding the classes out for the color, toggler, and collapsible, and with cards you have a title and content, and it's all wrapped inside a card. In the top piece, we are going build forms, and like a lot of our other sites, we are going to make this responsive. Similar to our previous projects, we will have two columns and at the bottom of the page we will have our footer. There are other sections in this site, such as Members, Groups, Photos, and Profile. We won't be going into the details on the Members, Groups, and Profile sections because once you see how the Home section is put together, you'll know how to build these too. We will, however, look at the Photos section mainly because it's got a lightbox, so we're going to see how to integrate that into the site too. So, let's go ahead and jump into our social media website.

The topics that we are going to cover are:

- Creating the header layout for the Home page
- Creating navigation and wall comments
- Creating styling bubble comments
- Creating the My Friends section
- Creating the Latest Groups section
- Creating the footer section
- Creating the Photos section

Creating the header layout for the Home page

In this section, we are going to create the top structure where we have our logo on the left and form fields on the right. The following is what we are going to build:

Let's go ahead and get into VS Code and start working on the site. First, we need to import the template into our project. Open your integrated terminal and just do `ls`. We want to make sure we are in the root folder because sometimes the integrated terminal might be in a different directory, so you always want to make sure you're in the same folder. To start, we are going to remove `Hello, world!` from our `index.html`, which came as a template, and we're going to start creating that top structure.

We're going to get a `div` tag with `class="container"`, and start wrapping everything inside of this container. We're going to have `class="row"` and now we're going to separate these out. So, we're going to do a 4 on one side and that's going to be for the medium, and we're also going to bring in a large, which is going to be a column of 6. So, we're going to have 4 and 8 for the mediums, and then 6 and 6 for the large. That's how these columns are going to be divided up depending on their breakpoints:

```
<div class="container">
  <div class="row">
    <div class="col-md-4 col-lg-6">
    </div>
    <div class="col-md-8 col-lg-6">
    </div>
```

The first column is going to be fairly easy to do. We are going to get the logo for our site, which is `img/logo.png`, and we're going to have a class called `img-fluid` from Bootstrap, and save it. Here is the code:

```
<div class="col-md-4 col-lg-6">
    <img src="img/logo.png" class="img-fluid">
</div>
```

Now we're going to get into the more complex part of this `header` section, which is going to be on the other side. Let's look at it:

```
<div class="col-md-8 col-lg-6">
  <form class="form-inline">
    <div class="form-group">
      <div class="form-group">
        <label for="exampleinputemail3">Email address</label>
        <input type="email" class="form-control"
        id="exampleinputemail3" placeholder="Enter email">
      </div>
      <div class="form-group">
        <label for="exampleinputpassword3">Password</label>
        <input type="password" class="form-control"
        id="exampleinputpassword3" placeholder="Enter password">
      </div>
```

```
    </div>
  </form>
</div>
```

We are going to have a `form` tag and our class is going to be `form-inline`. So, `form-inline` is actually because the form is all on one line, and it is coming out of Bootstrap. So the other `form` classes that we have added are also coming out of Bootstrap. We have our `form-group` as well, and then to further refine the spacing, we're going to add another `form-group` and we're going to add in some custom styling. It's going to help space out the `form` items a little bit. So, we'll toggle `form-group` and we'll see how they work when we get into the browser. We're going to add a `for` label and we're going to give this a name: `exampleinputemail3`. Then we add the `Email address` label. Now we will add an input, where `type` is going to be `email`, and the class is going to be `form-control`. Again, that's coming out of Bootstrap and just helps with styling on `form-control`. And then for our `id`, we are going to take the `exampleinputemail3` name and add it there. We're going to add a placeholder, which is `Enter email`. This group is going to end right here. Now we are going to copy the `form-group` we just created and use it for our password. The preceding code is self-explanatory. We have changed the names accordingly, the rest remains the same. Let's save and run the `gulp` command in our terminal. We can see the following in our browser:

This is the form at the top that we just created. Obviously there is no styling so we're just going to start bringing a little bit of that in. Before we go ahead with styling, make sure that the container we created for the top section is wrapped within the `header` tag. Let's go to our `style.scss` page now and start with styling. Remove anything that you have inside the Sass file; we're going to style against our `header` tag now:

```
header {
    background-image:linear-gradient(#04519b, #044687 60%, #033769);
    color:white;
    padding: 1rem 0;

    .form-group{
        display:flex;
        @media(max-width: 575px){
            margin-bottom: .25rem;
        }
    }
    .btn-light{
```

```
        height: 2.375rem;
    }
}
```

So, to set the background, we're going to have background-image, which is going to be linear gradient. If you check the final product of the header shown at the start of the section, the color blue is light at the top and gets darker toward the bottom, so that's what we're working on. To achieve that, we need a few different values for linear-gradeint. Then we add color: white for any text, and we're going to have a padding on this too, 1rem and 0; this shorthand targets the top and the right padding. Next, we target our form-group, and in here we're going to have display as flex. Then we add a breakpoint with max-width of 575px. Since the form is inline, it can do some weird stuff, so we're going to control that with this @media breakpoint, and we will have margin-bottom, which is very small, .25rem.

We also added a style to our btn-light class, which we don't have just yet, but we're going to add it shortly to our **Sign in** button. So on our button we have added a height of 2.375rem:

```
.form-group{
    padding:0 .125rem;
}
```

Before we go and create the Sign in button, we have one more class to add style to, that is our form-group. This will come outside our header. We have added padding to it on the top and right. Okay, now in our index.html file, we will create our button and the Remember me checkbox:

```
<div class="form-group">
    <label class="sr-only" for="exampleinputpassword3">Password</label>
    <input type="password" class="form-control"
    id="exampleinputpassword3" placeholder="Enter password">
</div>
    <button type="submit" class="btn btn-light">Sign in</button>
</div>
<div class="checkbox">
    <label>
        <input type="checkbox">Remember me
    </label>
</div>
```

Alright, so the button is going to go below this password code we created. It has
`type="submit"` and we also have `btn` and `btn-light` as our classes for the button. We
already customized our `btn-light` a while ago in our `style.scss` file. Finally, we named
the button **Sign in**.

Next we have the checkbox, so we added a `div` tag with checkbox as the class. Inside the
`div` tag, we added a `label` tag, and inside it we added an `input` tag, where
`type="checkbox"`, and named it `Remember me`. Before we go ahead and check it out on
the browser, let's add styles to our `checkbox` class:

```
.checkbox{
    float:left;
    width:100%;
    label{
        justify-content: left;
    }
}
```

We are done with the styling now. Let's save. Run `gulp` in the terminal and let's see how it
turns out:

So, we can see that it's starting to come out a little bit better. On the right side, you can see
it's getting clipped. Make sure we have all three CSS files in our project, that is,
the `bootstrap.css`, `font-awesome.css`, and `style.css` files, and also check for the `js`
files, which are Bootstrap, jQuery, and tether. To fix this, we are going to make a small
change to our code. We are going to add the `sr-only` class to our `label` tags, as follows:

```
<div class="form-group">
  <label class="sr-only" for="exampleinputemail3">Email address</label>
  <input type="email" class="form-control" id="exampleinputemail3"
  placeholder="Enter email">
</div>
<div class="form-group">
  <label class="sr-only" for="exampleinputpassword3">Password</label>
  <input type="password" class="form-control"
  id="exampleinputpassword3" placeholder="Enter password">
</div>
```

Earlier, the labels were coming through on our site because the right side was getting slipped. `sr-only` stands for screen reader only; it hides information intended only for screen readers. Now if we save and run, we will only see the input fields with the placeholders. As we already have the placeholders, having labels makes it redundant. Let's go ahead and check it out:

There you go, we have finally managed to get it right. Now that we are done with this section, we will go ahead and create our navigation bar.

Creating navigation and wall comments

Now we are going to build our navigation bar, which is below the header we just created in the previous section. Before we move ahead, let's look at the navigation bar that we are going to create:

We already created a navigation bar in Chapter 3, *Photosharing Website*. This is going to be somewhat similar. Here is the code:

```
<nav class="navbar navbar-expand-md navbar-light bg-light">
  <div class="container">
    <button class="navbar-toggler" type="button" data-toggle="collapse"
    data-target="#navbarsExample09" aria-controls="navbarsExample09"
    aria-expanded="false" aria-label="Toggle navigation">
      <span class="navbar-toggler-icon"></span>
    </button>
  </div>
</nav>
```

Now let's get into building out our navigation. So we have created a `nav` tag and it will have several classes that are fairly common in Bootstrap for navigation. We're going to have `navbar`, then `navbar-expand-md`, because we are working with that medium-sized screen, `navbar-light`, and we're going to have `bg-light`, which makes our background light as well. Now for the elements, we're going to start off with `class="container"` and this lets us know that we're going to be adding additional elements within the container and it is going to really keep everything responsive and not bleeding off the edges. Next, for our button we're going to have `navbar-toggler` and the type is just going to be `button`, and we have added data-toggle as collapse to make this thing work. Next, our data-target is going to be `#navbarsExample09`. Then we have our aria-controls, which are going to be the same, `navbarsExample09`, and we need `aria-expanded`, which we will keep as `false`, and finally `aria-label`, which is going to be `Toggle navigation`. These are our interactive components provided by Bootstrap 4. Now let's close the button tag and add an icon. We also added a `span` class that we're going to use, `navbar-toggle-icon`, and we're going to see shortly how this comes into play. Now we have to add content to our navigation bar.

We are still inside our `div` container, but we're right below our button. Let's look at the code for our navigation bar content:

```
<div class="collapse navbar-collapse" id="navbarsExample09">
  <ul class="nav navbar-nav">
    <li class="active">
      <a href="index.html" class="nav-link">Home</a>
    </li>
    <li>
      <a href="members.html" class="nav-link">Members</a>
    </li>
    <li>
      <a href="groups.html" class="nav-link">Groups</a>
    </li>
    <li>
      <a href="photos.html" class="nav-link">Photos</a>
    </li>
    <li>
      <a href="profile.html" class="nav-link">Profile</a>
    </li>
  </ul>
</div>
```

So, we're going to start with another `div`. We have added the `collapse` and `navbar-collapse` classes, and we gave `id="navbarsExample09"`, this is the `id` that we targeted previously, and we'll close that off. Now we can start creating the particular elements inside of this `div`. We have created an unordered list where we have `nav` and `navbar-nav` classes. You can see we started all these chained classes off with `nav`, which is the base, then we start getting in the particular kinds that we want. Next we have our `li` tags, so our first in the list is going to be our Home page. We will link it to our `index.html` file and it has a `nav-link` class, which comes out from Bootstrap. We are going to make our first link active, so we have added the `active` class. The remaining elements in the list are basically a copy of this; just make sure you rename them and you don't have the `active` class added to the rest. Once we have our Members, Groups, Photos, and Profile linked to their respective pages, our navigation bar should be complete. So, let's save and see what we have:

There you go, we have our navigation section ready. Currently, there's no toggling, these are just laid out flat, non-dynamic, so the toggling comes in when you get responsive, so you get what's called the hamburger menu. Let's resize the browser to see the toggling:

Creating wall comments

In the previous section, we completed our navigation bar. Before we start working on the wall comments, let's look at what we are going to build:

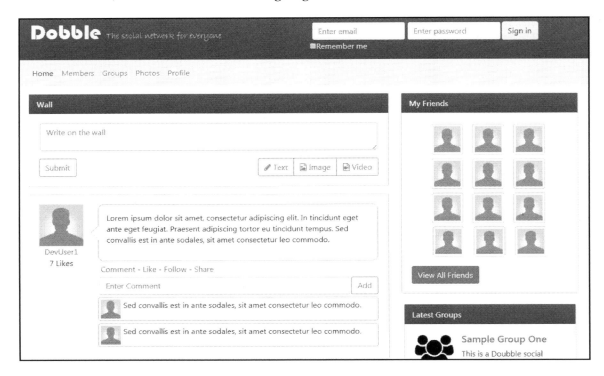

As we progress through this particular project, we can see the right side is actually going to be repeating across all different pages, such as Members and Groups. So, as we get into these other pages, which are less complex, we're going to go pretty quick and we're not going to do every single thing on these pages, although we will see how to create the lightbox under the Photos page.

As you can see in our previous screenshot, we are going to build the wall, which is on the left, and below that, you can see the users are actually leaving comments, which we will be covering in here. The wall is basically made of cards, so let's look at the code now:

```
<section>
  <div class="container">
    <div class="row">

        <div class="col-lg-8">
            <div class="card">
            <div class="card-heading">
            <h6 class="card-title">Wall</h6>
        </div>
        <div class="card-body">
            <form>
              <div class="form-group">
                <textarea class="form-control" placeholder="Write on
                the wall"></textarea>
              </div>
                <button type="submit" class="btn btn-outline
                secondary">Submit</button>
              <div class="float-right">
                <div class="btn-group">
                </div>
```

We are going to start with `section`, where we're going to have a `div` tag with `class="container"`. This follows a similar pattern to what we've been using, and we're going to start creating our rows and columns. The column we are going to work on is on the left side of our site, which is going to be `col-lg-8`. Now we start creating our cards. So we're going to have a class that's going to be `card`, which is the root of our cards, and then we're going to add another `div` with class as `card-heading`. Close that div. Now we've got a heading, so in the heading where the Wall goes, we're going to have an `h6` tag where `class="card-title"`, so you can clearly see the hierarchy that's getting created with this card. This is the header information for our card. Now we want to create the body. So, next we create another div with `class="card-body"` and within it we have a `form` tag and we're going to create a `form-group` for the elements within this form. So, the first part of this is to create a large textbox to write on the wall. That's going to be a `textarea` and it's going to have a `form-control` class coming right from Bootstrap. We're going to have a placeholder, which is going to say `Write on the Wall`, then we want a button so we can submit the text. For our button, we're going to have `type="submit"`, and now we're going to create the styling by adding the `btn` and `btn-outline-secondary` classes, which are coming out of Bootstrap. We always start with our base class, in this case `btn`, then we can add the particular kind of styling that we want. Finally, add the button name as **Submit**. So, we can go ahead and take a look at what we have so far:

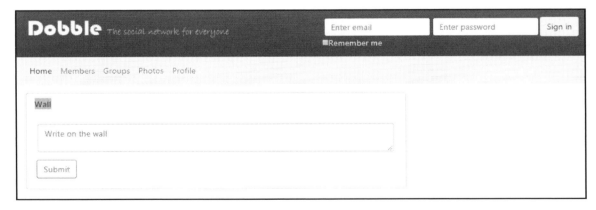

Now we're going to create those buttons on the bottom-right. So, we have a little bit of Sass that we need to introduce to make everything look right. Directly below our **Submit** button is where we're going to continue writing our code:

```
<form>
  <div class="form-group">
    <textarea class="form-control" placeholder="Write on the wall">
    </textarea>
  </div>
```

```
<button type="submit" class="btn btn-outline
secondary">Submit</button>
<div class="float-right">
  <div class="btn-group">
    <button type="button" class="btn btn-outline-secondary">
      <i class="fa fa-pencil"></i> Text</button>
    <button type="button" class="btn btn-outline-secondary">
      <i class="fa fa-file-image-o"></i> Image</button>
    <button type="button" class="btn btn-outline-secondary">
      <i class="fa fa-file-video-o"></i> Video</button>
  </div>
</div>
</form>
```

We are going to create a `div` tag with `class="float-right"`. Earlier, it was a class called `pull-right`, but now in Bootstrap 4, it's called `float-right`. We are then going to create another `div` tag with a class of `btn-group`. That's how we're able to make all these different buttons group together. We then create the particular kinds of buttons and each one of these is in fact a button, and there's a little bit more styling here; hence, we have added class. Again we start with the `btn` base class, then the kind. For our project, they're all going to be `btn-outline-secondary`, and then inside of our button, we create the italics tag, which is going to have the Font Awesome class. For the three buttons that we are going to create, each will have a different Font Awesome class but each will have the `fa` base class. For the Text button, we want a pencil icon, so we added the `fa-pencil` class. For the **Image** button, we have the `fa-file-image-o` class, and for the Video button we have the `fa-file-video-o` class. The rest of the code is the same for all three buttons. Alright, so now let's go to our website. We can see the buttons came out as expected:

Okay, so now we need to go into our Sass and do some styling. Here is the code:

```
.navbar{
    margin-bottom:1rem;
}

.card {
    margin-bottom:1rem;
}

.card-heading {
    background-image:linear-gradient(#04519b, #044687 60%, #033769);
    color:white;
    padding:.75rem 1rem;
    .card-title {
        margin-bottom:0;
    }
}
```

The preceding Sass code is pretty self-explanatory. We have added styling to our `navbar` and `card`. Let's save and see the result on our browser:

In the next section, we are going to create the bubble comment.

Creating and styling bubble comments

Now that we are done with the wall comments, let's go ahead and create the bubble comments section. We will have to create a new `card`, so let's go back into our `index.html` file. Now we're creating the card post, which is going to be inside the section, but not inside `card`. So, I'm going to collapse the card we just created for our wall because we're going to create another `card`. Here is the code:

```
<div class="card post">
  <div class="card-body">
    <div class="row">
      <div class="col-sm-2">
        <a class="post-avatar thumbnail" href="profile.html">
          <img src="img/user.png" class="img-fluid">
          <div class="text-center">DevUser1</div>
        </a>
        <div class="likes text-center">7 Likes</div>
    </div>
```

We are now inside our large column with span 8. Just to keep track of things, we will also create the other side column with span 4, which we will come back to later. Now we have added a new `div` tag with `class="card post"`. Next, we add one more `div` tag with a class of `card-body`, and in here we're going to have two columns for the small size. One is `col-sm-2` and the other is `col-sm-10`. In the `sm-2` column, we are going have the thumbnail of our avatar, username, and number of likes. We add an anchor tag with `class="post-avatar thumbnail"` and `href="profile-html"`. Inside the anchor tag, we add the user image and the `img-fluid` class, which is coming out of Bootstrap. Now we want our username to be center-aligned so we have added the `text-center` class. Outside the anchor tag, we have added 7 `Likes` inside a `div` tag with the same class for center alignment. So, this was one side, let's take a look at our site:

So, here we are. This is shaping up to look very close to what we wanted. Now we're going to build out the section on the right side. Let's get into our bubble and the comments part. So, under this `sm-10` column, we are going to add the following code:

```
<div class="col-sm-10">
  <div class="bubble">
    <div class="pointer">
      <p>Lorem ipsum dolor sit amet, consectetur adipiscing elit. In
      tincidunt eget ante eget feugiat. Praesent
      adipiscing tortor eu tincidunt tempus. Sed convallis est in ante
      sodales, sit amet consectetur leo commodo. </p>
    </div>
    <div class="pointer-border"></div>
  </div>
```

We have created a `div` tag where our class is going to be `bubble`, and then we start building out the content inside it. So, we added a class of the `pointer` type followed by a paragraph with some `Lorem ipsum`. Below our `div` we are going to add another class for the border, `pointer-border`. After the bubble code, just add a comment saying something like `bubble code end` as a best practice so that it's easier for you to read the code. Let's save and look at the browser:

Lorem ipsum dolor sit amet, consectetur adipiscing elit. In tincidunt eget ante eget feugiat. Praesent adipiscing tortor eu tincidunt tempus. Sed convallis est in ante sodales, sit amet consectetur leo commodo.

DevUser1

7 Likes

It looks pretty neat. Now we're going to add in the comment before we end this particular section. So we're still inside our columns. Let's see the code:

```
<div class="comment-form">
  <form class="form-inline">
    <div class="form-group">
      <input type="text" class="form-control" id="exampleInputName2"
      placeholder="Enter Comment">
    </div>
  </form>
</div>
```

We created a div tag that is going to have a class for comment-form, and we're going to have form here. In here, we're going to style it up as form-inline, as we did earlier, and then we want to create a div and group our form items with class="form-group". Next, we've got an input type="text", and it will have form-control as our class. We will give it an id="exampleInputName2"—you can give it whatever name you want. Then we end it with a placeholder, which is going to be Enter comment, and that completes our input and form. Again, add a comment saying comment form end after the comment form code as a best practice. Let's save and take a look at it now:

Alright, so there we are. We still have a quite a bit of work to do. Now we are going to create the bubble that appears around the comment, as seen in the following target screenshot:

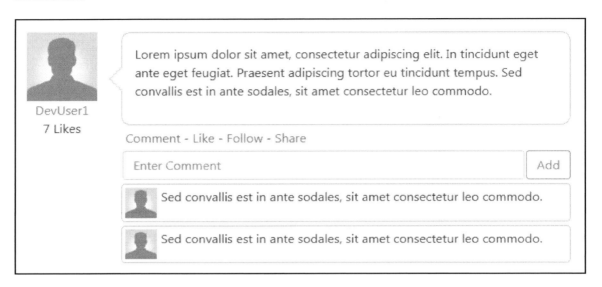

Once that is done, we have to add the **Comment - Like - Follow - Share** links, the **Add** button to submit our comment, and finally the two comments. Let's go to our Sass file now. The first thing we're going to do is create the root bubble, then we're going to work on some content using after and before selectors on our bubble. Here is the style code for our `bubble`:

```
.bubble {
    position: relative;
    min-height: 4rem;
    padding:1rem;
    background:#fff;
    border-radius: .75rem;
    border:1px solid #ccc;
}
```

So, we have a `bubble` class here. You should be familiar with most of the styles, except for `border-radius`, which is used for curved edges, and we have added a border of `1px` which is solid and light gray in color. If you save and check the comment now on our browser, you will see a rectangle around the comment with curved edges. But we want to work on the left side of our bubble now where we see a pointy pattern. So let's go ahead and work on the after and before selectors. Here is the code for `bubble:after`:

```
.bubble:after{
    content: '';
    position: absolute;
    border-style: solid;
    border-width: 15px 15px 15px 0;
    border-color: transparent white;
    display:block;
    width:0;
    z-index: 1;
    margin-top:-15px;
    left:-15px;
    top:50%;
}
```

Now this `after` selector works with the content, so we're going to use content with single quotes, and it will be empty, but you're going to see the effect it's going to have. We have the `position` as `absolute`, which is going to be relative and not static. We have added `z-index`, which is similar to three-dimensional coordinates, so you have an x, y, and z axis that you're working with. We have set it to `1`, this will help us with tilting. The rest of the style is easy to follow. Now we will look at the `before` selector code:

```
.bubble:before {
    content: '';
    position: absolute;
    border-style: solid;
    border-width: 15px 15px 15px 0;
    border-color: transparent #ccc;
    display:block;
    width:0;
    z-index:0;
    margin-top:-15px;
    left:-16px;
    top:50%;
}
```

Again, we are working with the content. Most of the styles are similar to the after selector except for a few things such as `z-index` and `left`, which is set to `-16px` to offset enough. The width and margins are set to odd numbers to create that particular effect with that triangle tilted the way that it is. Let's save and check how it looks now:

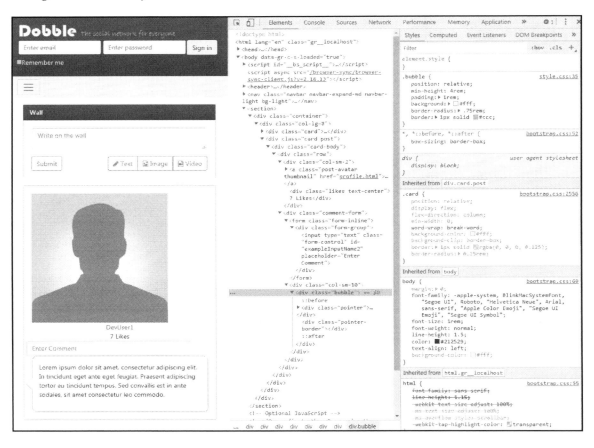

As you can see, we did a good job to create the bubble around the comment. I would suggest you right-click on the bubble comment and inspect it. As you can see in the preceding screenshot, you can play around with the styles on the right side of the **Elements** panel to understand how each property is affecting the bubble.

Now let's go back to our Sass file and add styles to our comments section. Here is the code:

```
.comment-form .form-group {
    width: calc(100% - 56px);
    margin-bottom:0;
}
```

```css
.comment-form input[type='text']{
    width: 100%;
}

.comment-avatar img {
    width:2.5rem;
    margin-right: .313rem;
}

.comment {
    border: 1px solid #ccc;
    border-radius: .313rem;
    padding: .25rem;
    margin: .313rem 0;
    overflow:auto;
    width:100%;
}
```

So we started off with the `comment-form` class and also `form-group`. We have added a width and are going to do a calculation in CSS, so we have `calc(100 -56px)`. This always subtracts `56px` from the `100%` width, which can change as the browser width changes. Then we have `margin-bottom`, which is set to `0`. Next, we added another `comment-form`, and this time we're going to work on our `input` tag, and specifically want it to be `type='text'`, as that's how you target a particular item, and are going to give a `width` of `100%`. Then we have our regular comment class. So, again, the numbers used for styling it are just trial and error, because you can tell whether you want a big margin or a small margin, then once you decide which way to go, if it's small you start dialing it in until you reach the point that you want. You can save and go to the finished product, but there's not as much going on there right now. We have to do a little bit more build out, so we're going to go back into our `index` file and see where we left off.

Now we have to add the two comments, so we will start right after where `comment-form` ended. Remember we have added comments so that we know where a particular code started and ended. Here is the code:

```html
<!-- comment form end -->
<div class="clearfix"></div>
<div class="comments">
  <div class="comment">
    <a class="comment-avatar pull-left" href="#">
      <img src="img/user.png" class="img-fluid">
    </a>
    <div class="comment-text">
      <p>Sed convallis est in ante sodales, sit amet consectetur leo
      commodo.</p>
```

```
        </div>
      </div>
    <div class="clearfix"></div>
```

We have added a `div` tag and it has `class="clearfix"`, and we are going to start with our comments. We created another `div` and our class that we have created is called `comments`. Inside it, we added one more `div`, with `class="comment"`, and now we start building out. Next, we have our `href`, which is going to have `comment-avatar` and `float-left` as classes, and again that's a replacement of the older `pull-left`. So, the image for our `comment-avatar` is going to be `src="img/user.png"`, and we'll go with `class="img-fluid"`. Then we added text for our comment, so we'll have our class, which is going to be `comment-text`, we need a paragraph of `Lorem ipsum`; we will keep it short. Underneath this `div`, we are going to add one more `div` with `class="clearfix"`. Now, when to use the reset, the `clearfix`, is if you see some of the items from above bleeding over into classes below, you would use it, and I know that's going to be the case so that's why it's being used here. Now let's go ahead and take a look at where we are:

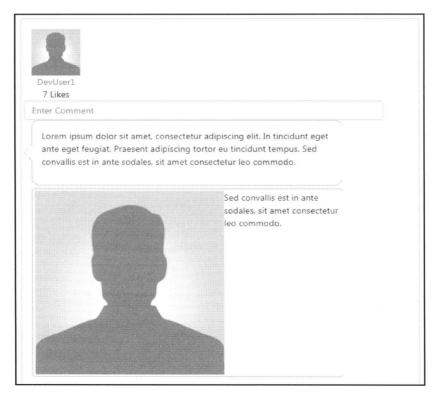

So, we can see here the image is quite big. We're going to fix that now with this last piece of styling, and there are a couple of classes we need to actually remove inside our HTML that we don't have. Let's look at the Sass code to reduce the size of our `avatar`:

```
.comment-avatar img {
    width:2.5rem;
    margin-right: .313rem;
}
```

So, we're going to have our `comment-avatar` on the image and we're going to take the width and bring it down to `2.5rem`. We have a margin on the right side that's going to be `.313rem`. Now if you save and check the browser, you should see the following output:

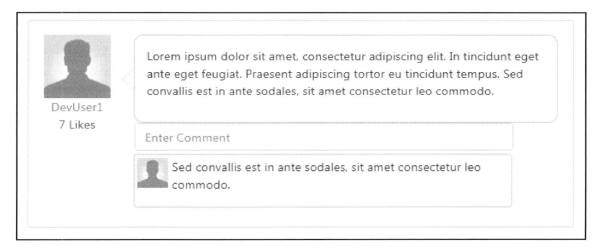

In the index file, we had added two classes, `comment-text` and `comments`, which we don't require, so we will remove them. Now we are left with the `Comment`, `Like`, `Follow`, and `Share` links and the **Add** button. Alright, now after the code where the bubble ends, we are going to add the code for our links:

```
<p class="post-actions">
  <a href="#">Comment</a> -
  <a href="#">Like</a> -
  <a href="#">Follow</a> -
  <a href="#">Share</a>
</p>
```

So we have added a paragraph tag with `class="post-actions"`, and `post-actions` is going to be one of ours. After that, we create `href` for each of the links: `Comment`, `Like`, `Follow`, and `Share`. Make sure you also add the hyphen as shown in the code because it acts as a separator on the page. Now we're going to add style in this class:

```
.post-actions {
    margin:.313rem;
}
```

So we have added a margin of `.313rem`, which is going to be on all sides. Let's save and take a look now:

So, there we are, we are still missing our `Add` button though, so let's start with it. Let's go to the `comment-form` section, right after the div tag where we have the `form-group` class. We are going to add in the code for our button. The code is as follows:

```
<form class="form-inline">
  <div class="form-group">
    <input type="text" class="form-control" id="exampleInputName2"
    placeholder="Enter Comment">
  </div>
  <button type="submit" class="btn btn-outline-secondary">Add</button>
</form>
```

There is nothing complicated in the button code we added. Let's save and go back to our site:

Everything looks good now. We have one more comment to add, but I will leave that for you to complete. It is a simple copy-paste. You can create a few more bubble comments and replies and fill up the left column of our Home page. We are done with our `column lg-8`. Let's go on to the other side to create our `Friends` section.

Creating the My Friends section

In the previous section, we completed the left side of our page, which had the wall and bubble comments. Now we are going to start working on the right side, which will have our `Friends` and our `Groups` section. Before we proceed, let's look at the target site of what we are going to build:

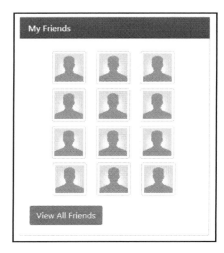

So, back into VS Code to work on the sidebar. Let's populate our `lg-4` column. Here is the code:

```html
<div class="col-lg-4">
  <div class="card friends">
    <div class="card-heading">
      <h6 class="card-title">My Friends</h6>
    </div>
    <div class="card-body">
      <ul class="list-inline">
        <li class="list-inline-item">
          <a class="thumbnail" href="profile.html">
            <img src="img/user.png" class="img-thumbnail">
          </a>
        </li>
        <li class="list-inline-item">
          <a class="thumbnail" href="profile.html">
            <img src="img/user.png" class="img-thumbnail">
          </a>
        </li>
</ul>
```

We're going to have a few more Sass classes that we're going to create. So, for this section, we are going to start off with a `card` and we're going to have a `friends` class, which is going to be one of ours. We then have a `div` tag with the `card-heading` class, and then we're going to have a title. For the title, it's going to be `h6` with a `card-title` class, and give it a title: `My Friends`. After that, we we are going to add one more div tag, and it will have the `card-body` class. This card body will have an unordered list with `class="list-inline"`, and then we're going to start adding the particular items, in our case thumbnails of our friends. So, we'll have our lists starting from here and it has `class="list-inline-item"`, and these are coming out of Bootstrap although we're going to add some of our styling on them. Next, we have an anchor tag that's going to have a class of `thumbnail`. We're going have `href` of `profile.html`, and inside it we will have our image, whose source is `img/user.png`, and we are going to style it with the `img-thumbnail` class. Now this was for one user who is your friend. We will have to create a few more, so let's make copies of the code we created and save it. If you go and check the browser now, you will see the thumbnails are large, so let's fix them using our Sass file. Here is the code:

```scss
.friends {
    margin: 0 -.313rem 1.4rem;

    .list-inline {
        text-align:center;
    }
}
```

```
li {
    margin:0;
    padding: .25rem .313rem;
}
img {
    width:4rem;
}
}
```

Now save, run `gulp`, and take a look at our site:

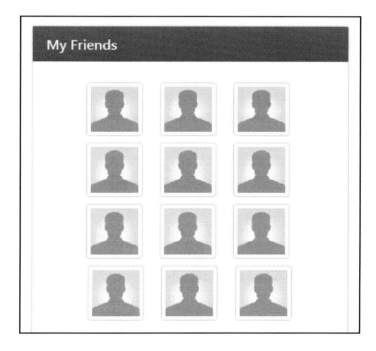

That came out to great! Now let's go ahead and create the **View All Friends** button. After the unordered list code, let's add our button:

```
<a class="btn btn-primary" href="#">View All Friends</a>
```

Let's save and look at our Friends section now:

There we go; our Friends section is ready. Now let's go ahead and create the Latest Groups section.

Creating the Latest Groups section

Let's jump into our VS Code and see how to implement the rest of this sidebar. Let's see what we are targeting:

We are going to add a card now. After the Friends section ends, we will add a new div tag and populate it with our code for our groups. Here is the code:

```
<div class="card groups">
  <div class="card-heading">
    <h6 class="card-title">Latest Groups</h6>
  </div>
  <div class="card-body">
    <div class="group-item">
      <img src="img/group.png" class="img-fluid">
      <h5><a href="#">Sample Group One</a></h5>
      <p>This is a Doubble social network sample group</p>
    </div>
<div class="clearfix"></div>
```

Inside the div tag, we have our class="cards groups". Then we have added one more div with the card-heading class. We then added an h6 header for our **Latest Groups** and also added the card-title class to it. Close the div and we will start creating our individual groups, for which we will create our card-body. Inside the card body, we have one more div with class="group-item". Now we will add our group image, give it a title of Sample Group One, and add a small description for it inside a paragraph tag. We created something similar earlier, so nothing new here. Finally, we will end the div tag with the clearfix class, so we don't have any bleeding into our remaining groups. Now the repetitive code is our group-item, so we will make copies of it and makes changes to it. Once our groups are created, let's create the button to view all our groups. Here is the code for that:

```
<a class="btn btn-primary" href="#">View All Groups</a>
```

We are done with the layout now. Let's go ahead and add some styling to fix the appearance. Here is the code:

```
.group-item{
    padding-bottom:.75rem;
    margin-bottom: 1.4rem;
    border-bottom: 1px solid #ccc;
    overflow:hidden;
}

.groups img{
    width:5rem;
    float:left;
    margin-right:1rem;
}
```

Let's save the file and check out our website:

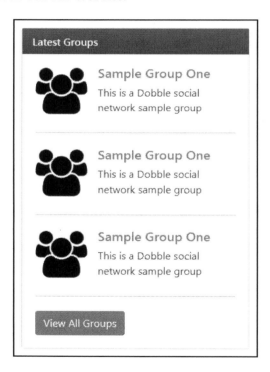

So there we are, we are done with our Groups section. Now let's create the footer section.

Creating the footer section

We already know what a footer is, so let's quickly go and create our `footer`. Here is the code:

```
<footer>
    <div class="container">
        <p>Dobble Copyright &copy; 2018, All Rights Reserved</p>
    </div>
</footer>
```

We also will need to add some CSS for this footer. There's not much to this part:

```
footer {
    background:#f4f4f4;
    height:5.75rem;
    color:#04519b;
    font-weight: bold;
    text-align: center;
    padding-top:2.5rem;
    margin-top:2rem;
    border-top:7px solid #04519b;
}
```

There isn't really anything complex going on here, just some minor aesthetics to get things looking the way we want, like the target site. Let's save it and look at our footer:

Dobble Copyright © 2018, All Rights Reserved

There we go, our footer is ready now. You can add this footer to our Home page as well. Now we are left with the Photos section.

Creating the Photos section

For the Photos page, we need `ekko-lightbox`. There are two ways to get `ekko-lightbox` into our project, one is using `npm` and the other is using CDN. For `npm`, you can run the following command on the terminal:

```
npm ekko-lightbox
```

For CDN, you can visit `https://cdnjs.com/libraries/ekko-lightbox`. From here, you will get the CSS and the js file. Since we have already done something similar earlier, we won't be covering it here now. We have already got `ekko-lightbox` into our project. As you can see, we have it in our `Project` folder:

We have got our CSS and js file and this is what's going to make our lightbox work. If you go to the bottom of the `index` file, you won't see anything new except for the JavaScript code:

```
<!-- Optional JavaScript -->
<!-- jQuery first, then Popper.js, then Bootstrap JS -->
<script src="js/jquery.min.js"></script>
<script src="js/popper.min.js"></script>
<script src="js/bootstrap.min.js"></script>
```

```
<script src="js/ekko-lightbox.min.js"></script>
<script>
  $(document).delegate('*[data-toggle="lightbox"]', 'click', function
  (event) {
  event.preventDefault();
  $(this).ekkoLightbox();
});
$(function () {
  $('[data-hover="tooltip"]').tooltip()
})
</script>
```

This JavaScript code is specific to `ekko-lightbox` to make it function because it targets a lot of different elements. We have `data-hover` and `data-toggle`, so you're going to see these attached to some of the photo items that we're going to be adding here shortly. We also have `ekko.lightbox.min.js` added to the script, as shown in the preceding code, and we have it added to our CSS as well:

```
<!-- Custom styles for this template -->
<link href="css/font-awesome.css" rel="stylesheet">
<link href="css/style.css" rel="stylesheet">
<link href="css/ekko-lightbox.css" rel="stylesheet">
```

We have set up most of the things that we require for our Photos page. You can find the working code for creating this page along with the book in the code repository. Also, in the last project that is Chapter 7, *Lightbox Website*, we are going to use lightbox to create something similar.

There are other pages too, such as Members, Groups, and Profile, and when compared to our Home page, they are very similar. I will leave these pages for you as an exercise.

Summary

In this chapter, we created a social media website. We saw how to create a navbar that had a brand and also a form field for the user to input their email address and password. We then created menu items that turn into a hamburger menu when shrinked. We also used cards to create our wall, friends, and groups section. We saw how to create a bubble comment and add an avatar. Finally, we learned how to get `ekko-lightbox` into our project to build the Photos page. In the next chapter, we are going to see how to create a one-page Bootstrap website.

6

Agency Website

In this chapter, we are now moving into our agency website project. This is going to be a one page responsive website. In this website, we will have navigation buttons where you will see effects when you hover the mouse over them. Since it's a one page website, clicking on a Menu item will automatically take you to the respective section on that page, which is basically an animation. This site will have different sections about the company such as why choose them, who they are, its clients, contacts, and finally the footer section. So, this is not going to be a complex site, but a pretty fun site to lay out.

In this chapter, we are going to cover the following topics:

- Creating the navigation bar and footer
- Creating the landing page
- Adding styles to the navigation bar and landing page
- Creating other sections about Digital Agency
- Creating JS code for scrolling animations

So, let's go ahead and jump in.

Creating the navigation bar and footer

So, the next website that we are going to build will be an agency website. Here, we are going to touch on some of the particular areas in Bootstrap 4 that we haven't really got into yet. Before we start coding, let's look at the website that we are going to build:

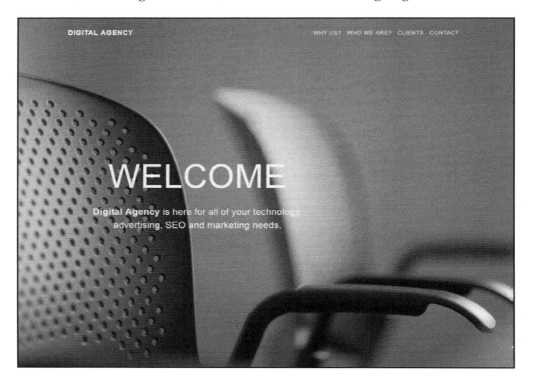

At the top, there is going to be the navigation. You can see the menu items are highlighted when we hover the mouse over them. The navigation seems to blend in with the page, but when we scroll down, you can see the menu changing a bit—it becomes darker:

When you scroll back, the menu changes to its original state. We also have the jumbotron introduction area that we're going to create.

So, let's go ahead and get into VS Code. The first thing that we have to do is get the template into our `index.html` file. We have also imported the images that we require for this site. Let's remove the `Hello, world!` which came with the template and add some styling into the `body` tag:

```
<body id="page-top" data-spy="scroll" data-target=".navbar-custom">
```

As you can see, the `data-spy` is actually part of the scrolling that we saw earlier. We're going to have a `data-target` as well, which is going to be `navbar-custom`. If you remember, `data-` is mainly related to accessibility. Now, we will start with our navigation:

```
<nav class="navbar navbar-expand-md navbar-custom navbar-dark fixed-top">
 <div class="container">
 <div class="page-scroll">
 <button class="navbar-toggler" type="button" data-toggle="collapse"
 data-target="#navbarsExample09" aria-controls="navbarsExample09"
 aria-expanded="false" aria-label="Toggle navigation">
 <span class="navbar-toggler-icon"></span>
 </button>
 <a class="navbar-brand" href="index.html">Digital Agency</a>
 </div>
```

So, we have a nav tag, which consists of several classes. The first one is our root, which is `navbar`, and it's going to be of type `expand`. We're targeting the medium here, which is a fairly safe one to target, and then we're going to go with `navbar-custom`, which is going to be one of our own, and will be created a little later. We then have `navbar-dark`, which is where the dark color comes from when we scroll down. Finally, we have `fixed-top` to make the navbar stick to the top. Next, we create a `div` tag with `class="container"` followed by one more `div` tag with `class="page-scroll"`, which is going to help us with the scrolling effect of the menu that we saw earlier. We are then going to have our button, which is going to be our hamburger menu. We have already created a hamburger menu several times before, so we know what the roles of these accessibilities are. Next, we created our icon, the visible part of that hamburger menu, which is going to have the `navbar-toggler-icon` class. Below the button, we're going to have another class, which is going to be a link, which is going to be the logo of our Digital Agency that you saw in the top left.

So, we have a `navbar-brand` class and we have added an `href` to `index.html`. Instead of using a picture for the logo, we have the text **DIGITAL AGENCY**. Finally, close this with the `div` tag.

Now, we are going to create the collapsible menu which was toward the top right-hand side. We are still inside our main `navbar` section, so let's see the code:

```
<div class="collapse navbar-collapse justify-content-end"
id="navbarsExample09">
 <ul class="nav navbar-nav ">
   <li class="hidden">
     <a href="#page-top" class="nav-link"></a>
   </li>
   <li class="page-scroll">
     <a href="#why" class="nav-link">Why Us?</a>
   </li>
   <li class="page-scroll">
     <a href="#who" class="nav-link">Who We Are?</a>
   </li>
   <li class="page-scroll">
     <a href="#clients" class="nav-link">Clients</a>
   </li>
   <li class="page-scroll">
     <a href="#contact" class="nav-link">Contact</a>
   </li>
 </ul>
 </div>
```

We have added a `div` tag with `class="collapse navbar-collapse justify-content-end`. Whenever we shrink the browser, we will get a hamburger menu, and when clicked, you will see the menu items expanded. We have added an `id`, which is basically telling us that the menu items that we are going to create belong to the hamburger menu icon we created earlier. Then, we created an unordered list for these various items. This needs a class, so we're still working with the `navbar`, that is, `nav` and `navbar-nav`. Now, we will start with the `li` tag, which will have a `hidden` class. We then have an anchor tag where `href` is going to be the `page-top` and the class is going to be a `nav-link` for obvious reasons. Since the rest of the links are going to be similar with a different class, we are going to copy paste them. The class for the other links is going to be `page-scroll`, and `href` is going to be `#why`, `#who`, `#clients`, and `#contact`, respectively. Now, we want to input our text, since these will be visible. These are going to be Why Us, Who We Are, Clients, and Contacts. This should complete our navigation. We are going to go ahead and take a look on our browser:

There you go, we have our navigation ready. Now, let's go ahead and finish off the footer, which is easy enough, and we'll do some minor styling. Here is the code:

```
<footer>
  <p>Digital Agency &copy; 2018, All Rights Reserved</p>
</footer>
```

As you can see, we have added our copyright text. Save that, and just take a look at how it looks now:

Digital Agency © 2018, All Rights Reserved

We definitely need to add some styling to it. Once the styling comes in, our footer will get fixed.

Creating the landing page

In this section, we're going to start off by creating the introduction section, which is our landing page. We will also be adding some of the Sass styling to our navigation, footer, and introduction section. Let's look at the code for our `intro` section:

```
<section class="intro">
 <div class="intro-body">
   <div class="container">
     <div class="row">
     <div class="col-lg-10 offset-lg-1 col-xl-8 offset-xl-2">
     <h1 class="brand-heading">Welcome</h1>
       <p class="intro-text">
       <strong>Digital Agency</strong> is here for all of your
       technology, advertising, SEO and marketing needs.</p>
   </div>
   </div>
  </div>
 </div>
</section>
```

So, we have created a section tag where our intro section code is going to be written. The `section` tag has a class called `intro`, which we will be using for styling purposes. For the same purpose, we have also added our `intro-body` class within a `div` tag. Then, we add our `container` class and `row`. After that comes the big area, basically like a jumbotron area that we saw earlier. We are going to use a little bit of offset while creating this. So, within the `div` tag, we have a class called `col-lg-10`. We are going to offset it with `offset-lg-1`. Remember we multiply the offset span value by 2, so in our case, it would be 2, as we are multiplying it with 1. 10 and 2 adds up to 12. Again, on the `xl`, we have `col-xl-8` and `offset-xl-2`, so 2 times 2 is 4; this too will add up to 12.

Alright, so now we're going to start working on the Welcome part of this section, which is going to be an `h1`. We're going to have a class called `brand-heading` to handle some of the styling. The next part we are going to be working on is our paragraph tag with our `intro-text`. We have added a sentence inside with the words **Digital Agency** in bold, so we put them within `strong` tags. That completes the introduction part. Let's look at the website:

Of course, it's going to need some styling, which we will cover in the next section.

Adding styles to the navigation and landing page

Let's jump into our Sass file now to fix it. The first thing that we are going to do is add in a few variables. Here they are:

```
$primary:#26a5d3;
$dark:#333;
$light:#f4f4f4;
```

Next, we are going to put in our code for the HTML and body:

```
html{
  width:100%;
  height:100%;
}

body{
  width:100%;
  height:100%;
  font-family:"Helvetica Neue", Helvetica, Arial, sans-serif;
  color:$dark;
  background-color:$light;
  overflow-x: hidden;
}
```

As you can see, in the body, the variables we created are getting used. There is nothing very complex going on here. We are going to see a lot of styling code now, but I will explain some of the more involved ones.

The Sass code for our typography is as follows:

```
h1, h2, h3, h4, h5, h6{
  margin: 0 0 2rem;
  text-transform:uppercase;
  font-family: "Montserrat","Helvetica Neue",Helvetica,Arial,sans-
  serif;
  letter-spacing:1px;
}

p{
  margin: 0 0 1.5rem;
}

a{
  color:$primary;

  &:hover,
  &:focus{
  text-decoration:none;
  color: darken($primary, 20%);

  }
}
```

We're keeping our heading tags all the same in regards to the fonts and spacing, and then there's a little bit of margin work that's going on for them as well. For our anchor tags, we had seen in the previous section that when we hovered the mouse over the menu items, they got highlighted with a darker background. So, to understand the syntax that we're using within the anchor tag, focus is targeting the text within the curly brackets, which is why you have this particular kind of syntax. We're setting our darken color based on a percentage, so we're using our variable for darken and we're just using 20 percent of it. You can see there's nothing on hover, so it could be removed, but it gives you an idea of what to do if you want to start chaining these, and particularly target something for hover. In that case, you would just put it inside your curly braces and start filling it in, the same way we did for focus. Basically, it's just going to do some targeting.

Now, let's go ahead and take care of the remaining CSS that we have for our navigation:

```
.navbar {
  margin-bottom: 0;
  border-bottom: 1px solid rgba(255,255,255,0.3);
  text-transform: uppercase;
  font-family: "Montserrat","Helvetica Neue",Helvetica,Arial,sans-serif;
  background-color: $dark;
}

.navbar-brand {
  font-weight: 700;
}

.navbar-brand:focus {
  outline: none;
}

.navbar-custom a {
  color: $light;
}

.navbar-custom .nav li a {
  -webkit-transition: background .3s ease-in-out;
  -moz-transition: background .3s ease-in-out;
  transition: background .3s ease-in-out;
}

.navbar-custom .nav li a:hover,
.navbar-custom .nav li a:focus,
.navbar-custom .nav li.active {
  outline: none;
  background-color: rgba(255,255,255,0.2);
}
```

```
.navbar-dark{
  .navbar-nav{
  .nav-link{color: white;}
  }
}
```

As you can see, CSS transitions are used. These are styles that are targeting different browsers. `-wekbkit` is for Chrome and Safari, whereas `-moz` is for Firefox. At the end of the preceding code, we can see a chain which is based on the hierarchy of `nav-link`. If you go and check our `index` page, you will see these classes nested in the order we see here. Let's go and get some more CSS for our project:

```
@media(min-width:767px) {
  .navbar {
  padding: 1.4rem 0;
  border-bottom: none;
  letter-spacing: 1px;
  background: transparent;
  -webkit-transition: background .5s ease-in-out,padding .5s ease-in-out;
  -moz-transition: background .5s ease-in-out,padding .5s ease-in-out;
  transition: background .5s ease-in-out,padding .5s ease-in-out;
}

.top-nav-collapse {
  padding: 0;
  background-color: $dark;
}

.navbar-custom.top-nav-collapse {
  border-bottom: 1px solid rgba(255,255,255,0.3);
  }
}

.page-scroll{
  -webkit-transition-property: -webkit-transform;
  -webkit-transition-duration: 1s;
  -moz-transition-property: -webkit-transform;
  -moz-transition-duration: 1s;
}
```

For our `navbar`, we are adding a breakpoint. We covered the role of having breakpoints entered manually earlier. We also have some colors and a border being added to our `navbar`. We have also added styling to our `page-scroll` class, which is again targeting the particular browser properties to make sure that the scrolling works as expected. Nothing complex is going on here, either.

Now, let's go ahead and bring in more CSS for our landing page:

```
.intro{
  display:table;
  width:100%;
  height:auto;
  padding:6rem 0;
  text-align:center;
  color:$light;
  background: url(../img/intro-bg.jpg) no-repeat bottom center scroll;
  background-color:$dark;
  -webkit-background-size:cover;
  -moz-background-size:cover;
  -o-background-size:cover;
  background-size:cover;
}

.intro-body{
  display:table-cell;
  vertical-align:middle;
}

.brand-heading{
  font-size:2.5rem;
}


.intro-text{
  font-size:1.1rem;
}

@media(min-width:767px) {
  .intro{
  height:100%;
  padding:0;
}

.brand-heading{
  font-size:6rem !important;
}

.intro-text{
  font-size:1.7rem;
  }
}
```

In the `intro`, we have `background`, where you can see we have our image for the landing page coming in. This is actually the main area that we are working on. Again, you can see that we have a little bit of work that's being done on the breakpoints just to ensure that we're getting the right kind of layout that we want and not using the particular default.

Now, we will check the styling on our `footer` section:

```
// Footer Section
footer{
  margin-top:.75rem;
  padding-top:2rem;
  height:80px;
  text-align:center;
}
```

There we go, nothing to explain here to either—we did something similar earlier. Let's save the file and go and check our website now:

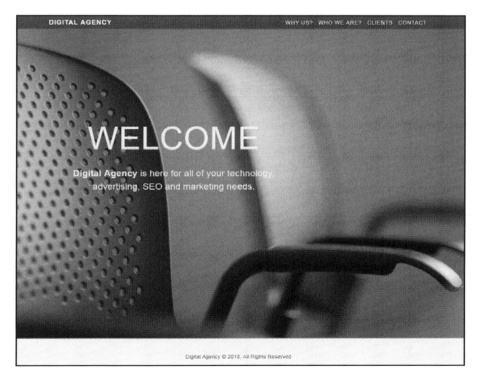

There we are, it came out pretty good. Now, in the next section, we are going to start working on the other sections.

Creating the WHY CHOOSE US? section

We have completed our navigation and intro page, so now we are moving on to the **WHY CHOOSE US** section. Let's look at what we are going to target:

As you can see, this section will require two rows to create this kind of layout. It is also using Font Awesome to get the icons. We have already seen a menu item named **WHY CHOOSE US?** in our navigation. If we click on it, you will see that the scrolling kicks in, which is kind of an animation, and you will be taken to this section. So, without further ado, let's get started. Let's go to our `index.html` and write the following code:

```
<section id="why" class="container content-section">
    <h2 class="text-center">Why Choose Us?</h2>
    <p class="text-center">Here are just a few reasons to choose
        <strong>Digital Agency</strong> for all of your digital marketing
        needs</p>
    <br>
    <div class="row">
        <div class="col-lg-4">
            <div class="block block-icon-left">
                <div class="icon">
                    <i class="fa fa-briefcase fa-5x"></i>
                </div>
                <div class="icon-content">
                    <h3>Professional</h3>
                    <p>Lorem ipsum dolor sit amet, consectetur adipiscing elit.
                    </p>
                </div>
            </div>
        </div>
    </div>
```

So, we start off with another section and give it an `id="why"`. It will also have a class of `container` and `content-section`, of which `content-section` is one of our classes that is in our Sass file. Next, we have our heading h2, **WHY CHOOSE US?**, and we have center aligned it using the `text-center` class. Then, we added a paragraph tag which has some text – this is center aligned too. Now, we will add some space with `<br>` tag and start creating our rows. We have six blocks, and they will be divided in three columns, each with a span of 4. Our column is going to be large, `col-lg-4`, and inside it we are going to add one more `div` tag with `class="block block-icon-left"`. Now, we will create another `div` tag with `icon` as a class. Inside it, we are going to use the italics tag, where we are going to use our Font Awesome. The first icon we are going to use is a briefcase, hence we have used `class="fa fa-briefcase fa-5x"`. Our icon is done, so now we have to add the content, which is basically the text. So, we will close the `div` tag which has our icon in it and create one more `div` tag that will have our heading h3 and a paragraph tag. Our heading will be `Professional` and the paragraph will include some `Lorem ipsum`.

Now, before we go and check our website, let's add some styling to our classes. Here is the Sass code:

```
// Content Section

.content-section{
  padding: 4rem 0 2rem;
}

// Icon Blocks

.block-icon-left{
  overflow:auto;

  h1, h2, h3, h4, h5, h6{
    margin:0 0 .75rem;
    padding:0;
    font-size: 1.4rem;
  }

  .icon-content{
    float:left;
    width:70%;
  }

  .icon{
    float:left;
    width: 30%;
    margin-top:.75rem;
```

```
      }
   }
```

This is pretty straightforward. As you can see, we have added padding to our `content-section` class. We have set our overflow to auto so that there is no clipping. We have also made some modifications to our headings and icon. Now, let's save the file and view our website:

Alright, it came out pretty good. Now, we have to do the same thing for our other blocks as well, so we will copy paste the code and modify the icon and icon content. Our next block is `Low Cost` and the code is as follows:

```html
<div class="col-lg-4">
  <div class="block block-icon-left">
    <div class="icon">
      <i class="fa fa-money fa-5x"></i>
    </div>
    <div class="icon-content">
      <h3>Low Cost</h3>
      <p>Lorem ipsum dolor sit amet, consectetur adipiscing elit.</p>
    </div>
  </div>
</div>
```

Our next block is `Fast` and the code for that is as follows:

```html
<div class="col-lg-4">
  <div class="block block-icon-left">
    <div class="icon">
      <i class="fa fa-dashboard fa-5x"></i>
    </div>
    <div class="icon-content">
      <h3>Fast</h3>
      <p>Lorem ipsum dolor sit amet, consectetur adipiscing elit.</p>
    </div>
```

```
    </div>
  </div>
```

As you may have noticed, each row has three blocks, so that would mean we will have to close the div tag with the row class now and create one more row. Now, let's go ahead and create the remaining three blocks. The first on the next row is Resources & Tools and the code for that is as follows:

```
<div class="row">
  <div class="col-lg-4">
    <div class="block block-icon-left">
      <div class="icon">
        <i class="fa fa-gear fa-5x"></i>
      </div>
      <div class="icon-content">
        <h3>Resources & Tools</h3>
        <p>Lorem ipsum dolor sit amet, consectetur adipiscing elit.</p>
      </div>
    </div>
  </div>
```

As you can see, we added one more row at the start of the code. Now, we will add the code for Large Community:

```
<div class="col-lg-4">
  <div class="block block-icon-left">
    <div class="icon">
      <i class="fa fa-users fa-5x"></i>
    </div>
    <div class="icon-content">
      <h3>Large Community</h3>
      <p>Lorem ipsum dolor sit amet, consectetur adipiscing elit.</p>
    </div>
  </div>
</div>
```

Now, we are going to do the same for the final block, which is Online Courses, and the code for that is as follows:

```
<div class="col-lg-4">
  <div class="block block-icon-left">
    <div class="icon">
      <i class="fa fa-book fa-5x"></i>
    </div>
    <div class="icon-content">
      <h3>Online Courses</h3>
      <p>Lorem ipsum dolor sit amet, consectetur adipiscing elit.</p>
```

```
        </div>
      </div>
    </div>
```

We are done adding all of the blocks, and we have added styles as well. Note that we have used different icons for different blocks with the help of Font Awesome. Now, let's save the file and go and check out our website:

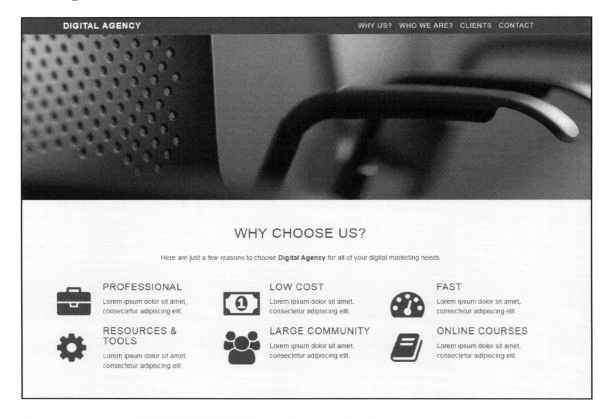

Here we are—our **WHY CHOOSE US** section is ready. You can always go back to our site and right-click and **Inspect elements** to see how each block of code or styles are affecting the page's layout.

Now, we have three more sections remaining, which are who we are, clients, and contact, which we will be covering in the next few sections.

Creating the WHO WE ARE section

Now, we're going to move on to our next section, which is the **WHO WE ARE** section. Let's look at what we are targeting:

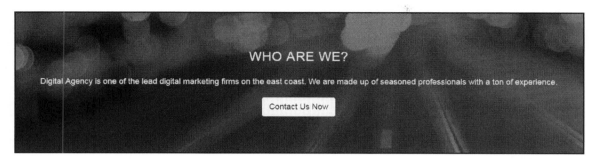

We will once again start with a `section` tag and give it an `id="who"`. Even if you're not using an `id`, especially in this case, you can demarcate sections of your site and just make it very easy to understand what's going on. This kind of acts as a little bit of metadata. Let's look at the code:

```
<section id="who" class="content-section text-center">
  <div class="who-section">
    <h2>Who We Are?</h2>
    <p class="lead">
      <strong>Digital Agency</strong> is one of the lead digital
      marketing firms on the east coast. We are made up of seasoned
      professionals with a ton of experience.</p>
    <a href="#contact" class="btn btn-light btn-lg">Contact Us
    Now</a>
  </div>
</section>
```

We have added `content-section` and `text-center` as our classes. We then created one more `div` tag with `class="who-section"`, which is one of our classes. We will look at it soon. Next, we have the heading `h2` with the text **WHO WE ARE**, followed by a paragraph tag which will have some text in it. Finally, we added a button named **Contact Us Now**, and used the Bootstrap class to style it. Now, let's look at the Sass file to see the styles that have been used for this section:

```
.who-section{
    width:100%;
    padding:3rem 0;
    color:$light;
    background: url(../img/downloads-bg.jpg) no-repeat center center
```

```
        scroll;
        background-color:$dark;
        -webkit-background-size:cover;
        -moz-background-size:cover;
        -o-background-size:cover;
        background-size:cover;
    }

    @media(min-width:767px) {
        .who-section{
            padding: 6rem 0;
        }
    }
```

As you can see, we have added some width, padding, and color to this section. We have getting our background image and we have also added a dark background color. We also have a few browser-specific properties that are getting set. Finally, we have added code for the breakpoint, too. Let's save the file and look at what our site looks like:

Perfect! Now, let's move on and create the **OUR CLIENTS** section.

Creating OUR CLIENTS section

Let's start with creating the **OUR CLIENTS** section now. In this section, we are going to have our client logos in one row. Let's look at what we are targeting:

Our clients

Similar to our previous sections, this will also start with a `section` tag and will have an `id="clients"`. Let's look at the code:

```
<section id="clients" class="content-section text-center">
    <div class="container">
      <h2>Our Clients</h2>
      <ul class="list-inline">
        <li class="list-inline-item"><img src="img/partner1.png"
        class="img-fluid" alt="img description"></li>
        <li class="list-inline-item"><img src="img/partner2.png"
        class="img-fluid" alt="img description"></li>
        <li class="list-inline-item"><img src="img/partner3.png"
        class="img-fluid" alt="img description"></li>
        <li class="list-inline-item"><img src="img/partner4.png"
        class="img-fluid" alt="img description"></li>
        <li class="list-inline-item"><img src="img/partner5.png"
        class="img-fluid" alt="img description"></li>
        <li class="list-inline-item"><img src="img/partner6.png"
        class="img-fluid" alt="img description"></li>
      </ul>
    </div>
  </section>
```

As you can see, we have created an unordered list within which we will list down our clients inline. We have a class called `list-inline` within our `ul` tag, which lists the items in one line. We then added list tags with the `ul` tag. Each one has a `class="list-inline-item"`. We then added the source of all six client's logos and added a `class="img-fluid"` for it to be responsive. Now, we will look at the Sass code for this section:

```
#clients{
    text-align:center;
    padding-bottom:5rem;

    .list-inline{
        letter-spacing: -6px;
        margin: 0 -1rem 1rem;

        li{
            letter-spacing: 0;
            padding: .5rem 1rem;
            vertical-align: middle;
        }
    }
}
```

Here, we have a class called `list-inline` and a list, `li`, nested with the ID `clients`. These follow the same hierarchy in the index file. Let's save it and look at our website now:

Our clients

Alright, so our client section is ready. We only have one more section remaining, and then we should be done with our agency website.

Creating the contact section

Similar to our previous sections, we will add another section where id="contact". Before we write the code, let's look at what we are going to create:

Let's create a section tag where id="contact". We have added both the content-section and text-center classes to it, as we have done for the other sections. Here is the code for our contact section:

```
<section id="contact" class="content-section text-center">
    <div class="row">
      <div class="col-lg-10 offset-lg-1 col-xl-8 offset-xl-2">
        <h2>Contact Digital Agency</h2>
        <p>Feel free to shoot us an email any time for any reason. You
        can also follow us on Twitter, Facebook and Google+</p>
        <p>contact@digitalagency.com</p>
        <ul class="list-inline banner-social-button">
          <li class="list-inline-item">
            <a href="#" class="btn btn-light btn-lg">
            <i class="fa fa-twitter fa-fw"></i>
            Twitter</a>
          </li>
          <li class="list-inline-item">
            <a href="#" class="btn btn-light btn-lg">
            <i class="fa fa-facebook fa-fw"></i>
            Facebook</a>
          </li>
```

```
        <li class="list-inline-item">
          <a href="#" class="btn btn-light btn-lg">
          <i class="fa fa-google-plus fa-fw"></i>
          Google+</a>
        </li>
      </ul>
    </div>
  </div>
</section>
```

As you can see, we have created a row and column similar to our intro page, so we should now be familiar with how `offset` works. Then, we added our heading in an `h2` tag and the description text within the paragraph tag, followed by one more paragraph tag containing the email address. Next, we added our social media buttons which are inline with the `ul` tag. We have added a `list-inline` class which we are already familiar with, and then we added one more class called `banner-social-button`, which is one of the classes we will look at shortly. For the buttons, we have added the `btn-light` and `btn-lg` classes to make it look white and large. To get the social media logos for Facebook, Twitter, and Google+, we have used Font Awesome. For Twitter, we have `fa-twitter`, for Facebook, we have `fa-facebook`, and for Google+, we have `fa-google-plus`. That's it! Now, let's quickly check the Sass part:

```
#contact{
    background:$dark;
    color:$light;
    padding-bottom:5rem;
}
```

We also added styles to our `banner-social-button` class. Here is the code for this:

```
.banner-social-buttons{
    letter-spacing: -6px;
    margin: 0 -.5rem 1rem;
    li{
        vertical-align: middle;
        margin: 0 !important;
        padding: 0 .5rem .5rem;
        letter-spacing: 0;

    }
}
```

The Sass code for this section is straightforward – nothing complicated going on over here. Now, let's save the file and check our browser:

With this, we are done with all the sections.

Creating JS code for scrolling animations

So, where did that come from, because it wasn't there before? Let's take a look at how that works. So, scrolling down, we have main.js. If I go and look in here, we have main.js. This right here is helping us with our scrolling, so I'm just going to go through and explain what this is because you can get this code to make this work off Stack Overflow.

So, if you search for bootstrap scrolling `navbar` issues, you will be able to scroll down and find it. If you look at the code being used, it's very similar to what I have. Let's take a look at our menu to see the functionality of how this actually works. When scrolling up, you get an animation which is using a plugin for jQuery. That is a lot of JavaScript running, along with this animation that we're seeing, and the easing in plugin, let's go look right here, `jquery.easing.min.js`, which if you do a search on that you will find it as well. You can actually search for that script. So let's see, I'm just going to show you how to get this one file and, put this in. There's a CDN so this is the one right here. You can go there and you'll see it in the CDNs, just download it right there. Okay, so going into our JavaScript here, our jQuery here, and again you need this file and just link it like I've linked it. All that is in the project when you download it. Okay, so what we're doing is kicking this off on a scroll, so we're looking, if we have `navbar`, for this offset, so offset gets coordinates, right here we're getting the coordinate just for top so that brings back just the coordinate, because usually with offset you'll get, or you will get top and left, so you get two of them. We're just getting one of them and we're saying greater than 50. We're going to add in this class, and we're going to take a look and we're actually going to see how it works, otherwise we're going to remove it. So, that's helping with our appearance, so now here's where the animation is. What we're doing is looking for page-scroll, the anchor tag, and we're going to put a click in there and then we're going to stop the animation, make this `scrollTop`, and you can see we're getting a coordinate just for the top on the anchor tag, and we're going to do a 1.5 second animation called `easeOut`, and then this right here, `event.preventDefault`, because we're attaching to an anchor tag, we're basically removing the default behaviour, which is to take you out to a website. So, let's go and look now at our site, and if we scroll down you can see the animation that we get right there. Now this 1.5 seconds, so if I click, that's 1.5 seconds. If I were to change this to 3,000, of course that's going to be 3 seconds, as it should be twice as long. So, let's take a look and I actually need to refresh to make that kick in. Alright, so scrolling back up here, if I click **CLIENTS**, notice it's a lot slower so I actually slowed it down whenever I did that, so that is how all of this is working. Now let's look where this comes in, this adding and removing of the class, and that is going to be in our menu. So, I'm just going to do an Inspect so that we can see that on here. Alright and let's see, we are up here, so notice we have top-nav-collapse is there. Now watch this class, watch what happens when I scroll up, it's gone, so that is what that Java, that jQuery is doing, it's removing it and adding it.

Now watch, it'll come back, there it is, because I've hit that 50, that it's looking for, that 50 pixels offset from the top. So, see I'm scrolling down, now I'm 50 from the top and it's there. I move back up, now it's not there, so that is how that works, and at this point we have completed our agency website. So, everything is in there that we were after, and we have the same kind of look minus the little bit of difference with the fonts because we're not using the Google API fonts, we're just making use of Font Awesome. So, now you have a great-looking layout for an agency site, this can be used for a lot of different sites. We've seen how to do this background, we've brought in as well this scrolling that we have up here, we've done a lot of work with Font Awesome icons, and again the alignment that we get out of those, so a lot of great new learning that we've added here in regards to Bootstrap 4. So, I hope you got a lot out of this particular project, some good additional tools for your toolbox, and again you'll get all the different code that we've gone over whenever you download the project.

Summary

Now, we shall start with the course and projects on Bootstrap 4. To summarize what we've learned in this agency project—we created the navigation at the top, we have the branding section, and we have the actual menu of items.

We can also shrink them up and get a responsive behaviour from it.

If we bring the pointer over to the navigation buttons, we get our hamburger icon, we get the menu items there, and then the responsive site—everything starts snapping into place into a single column, which is exactly what we'd expect. Along with the animation when scrolling manually, the item can also be clicked for the scrolling action to work. The menu will change, and we get the animation that will take us down into that area of the page that we are targeting. For example, if we have to go to the **CLIENTS**, all that needs to be done is scroll. This is going to use an offset which is going to grab the top coordinate of the offset. We used an anchor and brought in the Bootstrap button classes to do that. We also did a lot of work with Font Awesome, so we get to see its features. There is no need to put in extra efforts to search for icons the same can be done using Font Awesome's huge library of icons. With this we can close the quick summary of what we've covered in our agency website.

Lightbox Website 7

In this chapter, we're are going to build our PhotoShak project. This is going to be another kind of photo-sharing project like the one in Chapter 3, *Photosharing Website,* but this one will have a different layout and we will cover a few more Bootstrap features that we haven't seen yet. We will be creating a carousel, as well as tabs that will have content, in our case, images. We will be covering lightbox and the plugin that we are going to use for it. Let's start building our photo-sharing website.

The topics that we are going to cover are:

- Creating the carousel
- Creating the tabs
- Creating the three-column layout

Creating the carousel

Before we start coding our website, let's get the template for our new project. We also have the CSS for the lightbox file and the JS. So, we are ready to roll. The first thing we're going to do, as we usually do, is start with the navigation. You should be familiar with how to create it as it follows a particular kind of hierarchy. Let's look at what we are targeting:

So, we have our navigation bar and `carousel`. Here is the code for our navigation bar:

```
<nav class="navbar navbar-expand-md navbar-dark bg-dark fixed-top">
  <div class="container">
    <a class="navbar-brand" href="index.html">PhotoShak</a>
    <button class="navbar-toggler" type="button" data-toggle="collapse"
    data-target="#navbarsExample09" aria-controls="navbarsExample09"
    aria-expanded="false" aria-label="Toggle navigation">
      <span class="navbar-toggler-icon"></span>
    </button>
    <div class="collapse navbar-collapse" id="navbarsExample09">
      <ul class="nav navbar-nav">
        <li class="active">
          <a href="index.html" class="nav-link">3 Column Layout</a>
```

```
      </li>
      <li>
        <a href="index2.html" class="nav-link">4 Column Layout</a>
      </li>
    </ul>
  </div>
  </div>
</nav>
```

By looking at the code, you should be able to understand what we just did; it is self-explanatory. We have created a navigation bar with a dark color, which has `navbar-brand` as PhotoShak. We then created a hamburger menu, and two menu items: **3 Column Layout** and **4 Column Layout**.

Next, we will start working on our `carousel`. The code for it is as follows:

```
<section id="carousel">
    <div class="container">
      <div class="row">
        <div class="col-sm-12 col-md-12 col-lg-8 offset-lg-2 col-xl-6
        offset-xl-3">
          <div id="carouselExampleIndicators" class="carousel slide"
          data-ride="carousel">
            <ol class="carousel-indicators">
              <li data-target="#carouselExampleIndicators" data-
              slide-to="0" class="active"></li>
              <li data-target="#carouselExampleIndicators" data-
              slide-to="1"></li>
              <li data-target="#carouselExampleIndicators" data-
              slide-to="2"></li>
              <li data-target="#carouselExampleIndicators" data-
              slide-to="3"></li>
              <li data-target="#carouselExampleIndicators" data-
              slide-to="4"></li>
              <li data-target="#carouselExampleIndicators" data-
              slide-to="5"></li>
            </ol>
            <div class="carousel-inner" role="listbox">
              <div class="carousel-item active">
                <img class="d-block img-thunbnail"
                src="images/sample1.jpg" alt="img1">
              </div>
              <div class="carousel-item">
                <img class="d-block img-thunbnail"
                src="images/sample2.jpg" alt="img2">
              </div>
              <div class="carousel-item">
                <img class="d-block img-thunbnail"
```

```
                src="images/sample3.jpg" alt="img3">
            </div>
            <div class="carousel-item">
              <img class="d-block img-thunbnail"
                src="images/sample4.jpg" alt="img4">
            </div>
            <div class="carousel-item">
              <img class="d-block img-thunbnail"
                src="images/sample5.jpg" alt="img5">
            </div>
            <div class="carousel-item">
              <img class="d-block img-thunbnail"
                src="images/sample6.jpg" alt="img6">
            </div>
          </div>
          <a class="carousel-control-prev"
          href="#carouselExampleIndicators" role="button" data-
          slide="prev">
            <span class="carousel-control-prev-icon" aria-
            hidden="true"></span>
            <span class="sr-only">Previous</span>
          </a>
          <a class="carousel-control-next"
          href="#carouselExampleIndicators" role="button" data-
          slide="next">
            <span class="carousel-control-next-icon" aria-
            hidden="true"></span>
            <span class="sr-only">Next</span>
          </a>
        </div>
      </div>
    </div>
  </div>
</section>
```

For our `carousel`, we will start with the section tag and give it `id="carousel"`. This start is pretty similar to other sections we created in previous chapters. We have a `container` class followed by a row and then a column. In this project, we are going to define a column for all different sizes. For `sm` and `md`, we are going to have a span of `12`. For `lg`, we will have 8 and set the offset to 2, and for `xl`, we will have 6 and set the offset to 3. You should know why we have offsets and how they work.

Now we will start with the `carousel`. We are going to add a `div` tag where id is `carouselExampleIndicators`. The carousel does have a hierarchy and this is the main, top part of it. We then add `class="carousel slide"`, followed by `data-ride="carousel"`. `data-ride` tells Bootstrap to start animating as soon as the page loads. Next, we're going to have an ordered list. These are going to be for those indicators, the bars that we saw at the bottom of the `carousel`. The bar is highlighted when its respective image appears on the carousel. Then we will have our lists. Since we are going to add six images to our `carousel`, we will have to create six bars. So the `data-target` for each of them will be the same, that is, `#carouselExampleIndicators`. Then we have our `data-slide-to`, which we will set to 0, and we will keep the first one active, hence we have added the class. Now we will copy this list and paste it five more times as we are going to create six bars in total. Make sure the others are not set to active and the `data-slide-to` is serialized from 0 to 5, in that order. Now, close the ordered list and we are going to bring in the images to our `carousel`.

We will add a `div` tag with `class="carousel-inner"` and `role="listbox"`. Now, `carousel-inner` is going to add slides and `listbox` is basically telling us that there is more than one option to choose from in here. We then create one more `div` tag with `class="carousel-item"` and keep it `active`. Now, we add the image source, which is going to be active, within the `img` tag and use `class="d-block"`, which is basically a display block that we have seen earlier in one of our projects, and the `thumbnail` class, and `alt="img1"`, and close it off. Now we have to create five more carousel items, so we will make copies of this. Ensure you remove the active class from the others and provide the right source to the images. We are done adding the images now. Next we are going to add the controls, previous and next, which are going to be our anchor tags.

So we add an anchor tag for `class="carousel-control-prev"` and `href="carouselExampleIndicators"`. We then give it the role of a button, and the `data-slide` is set to `prev`. Then, we add a couple of spans, of which one is going to create the icon and the other is going to be the actual text. We then add `aria-hidden="true"` for the icon, and for the text we add the `sr-only` class, which is screen reader only. You will probably remember these. We are done with the previous button, now we will add the next button. So, we can just copy paste the code and replace `prev` with `next`, and we will be done with our `carousel`. Now, let's save the file and check our website:

Creating the tabs

In the previous section, we covered the navigation bar and the `carousel`. Now, we will be creating the tabs that will have all the images. This section will come just under the carousel that we created. Let's look at what we are targeting:

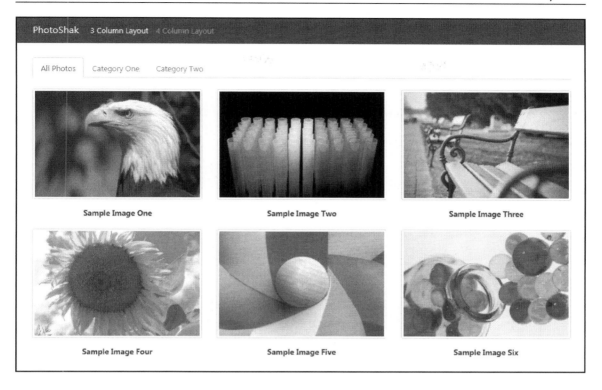

As you can see, we have three tabs, one that contains all the photos, and then these photos are categorized in the other two tabs. So, let's get started. In our Visual Studio Code, where the carousel section ends, we are going to add one more section tag and give it id="maintabs". Now, looking at the layout, we can see there are two rows, and in each row, we are going to have three columns. We are going to create the **All Photos** tab now, the other two tabs will follow the same approach. Let's look at the code for the tabs now:

```
<section id="maintabs">
    <div class="container">
      <div role="tabpanel">
      <ul class="nav nav-tabs" role="tablist">
        <li class="nav-item">
          <a href="#all" class="nav-link active" aria-controls="all"
          role="tab" data-toggle="tab">All Photos</a>
        </li>
        <li class="nav-item">
          <a href="#one" class="nav-link" aria-controls="one"
          role="tab" data-toggle="tab">Category One</a>
        </li>
        <li class="nav-item">
```

```
            <a href="#two" class="nav-link" aria-controls="two"
            role="tab" data-toggle="tab">Category Two</a>
        </li>
    </ul>
```

We have added a `container` class and then created one more `div` tag. We're going to use `tabpanel` to create the effect, and in here we're going to start creating our tabs, which are going to be unordered lists. So, we start with a `nav` class as the root on this unordered list followed by `nav-tabs`. The role is going to be `tablist`. We then have our list coming in, and this is going to be our particular item, so the class is going to be `nav-item`. Inside the list we have added our anchor tag, which will have `href="#all"` as we are creating the **All Photos** tab, and our class is going to be `nav-link`. This being the first one in a grouping, we're going to make it `active`, then we have our `aria-controls`, which is going to be `all` as well. Then we have given the `role` of a `tab`, and `data-toggle` is also going to be a `tab`, and we'll call this **All Photos**. So, now we have a pattern that we can make use of and there's only two more of these, so we are just going to paste it twice and rename some of the elements in these to their respective categories. Make sure you remove the `active` class from the other two tabs. Save it and check out how the tabs look:

Alright, we are done creating our tabs, now we will create the content for each of our tabs. Going back to Visual Studio, we can start building out the parts underneath it and I'm going to add a line break and get into the tab panes section.

Creating the three-column layout

We will first start with the content for our **All Photos** tab. Let's look at the code now:

```
<div class="tab-content">
        <div role="tabpanel" class="tab-pane active" id="all">
          <div class="row">
            <div class="col-md-4">
              <a href="images/sample1.jpg" data-lightbox="gallery"
              data-title="Sample Image One">
                <img src="images/sample1.jpg" class="img-thumbnail">
              </a>
              <div class="title">Sample Image One</div>
            </div>
```

We have a `div` tag with `tab-content` as our class. We then added one more `div` tag with `id="all"` and set `role` to `tabpanel`. Since it's a pane, we are going to add `class="tab-pane"` and make it `active`. Now come the first row and column, so we are going to create a medium column, `col-md-4`. This column will contain our `anchor` tag, where we are going to reference the image that we need to display and add in our lightbox, so we will have our lightbox properties, where `data-lightbox="gallery"` and `data-title="Sample Image One"`. Next, inside the anchor tag, we are going to add the source of the image and, to give it a thumbnail look, we are going to add the `img-thumbnail` class. Finally, we will end this by giving the name that is going to be displayed on the screen, which is **Sample Image One**. Now, we have to add two more images for this row, which means adding two more columns, so the code is going to be the same except for renaming the elements that are going to be used, such as the image and title.

Here is the code for the other two images:

```
<div class="col-md-4">
            <a href="images/sample2.jpg" data-lightbox="gallery"
            data-title="Sample Image Two">
              <img src="images/sample2.jpg" class="img-thumbnail">
            </a>
            <div class="title">Sample Image Two</div>
        </div>
        <div class="col-md-4">
          <a href="images/sample3.jpg" data-lightbox="gallery"
          data-title="Sample Image Three">
            <img src="images/sample3.jpg" class="img-thumbnail">
          </a>
          <div class="title">Sample Image Three</div>
        </div>
```

There you go, we are done with one row. Now, we are going to do the same for the next row:

```
<div class="row">
            <div class="col-md-4">
              <a href="images/sample4.jpg" data-lightbox="gallery"
              data-title="Sample Image Four">
                <img src="images/sample4.jpg" class="img-thumbnail">
              </a>
              <div class="title">Sample Image Four</div>
            </div>
            <div class="col-md-4">
              <a href="images/sample5.jpg" data-lightbox="gallery"
              data-title="Sample Image Five">
                <img src="images/sample5.jpg" class="img-thumbnail">
              </a>
```

```
        <div class="title">Sample Image Five</div>
      </div>
      <div class="col-md-4">
        <a href="images/sample6.jpg" data-lightbox="gallery"
        data-title="Sample Image Six">
          <img src="images/sample6.jpg" class="img-thumbnail">
        </a>
        <div class="title">Sample Image Six</div>
      </div>
    </div>
```

Alright, there we are, we are done creating our first tab, which is the **All Photos** tab. Let's save the file and check how our website looks:

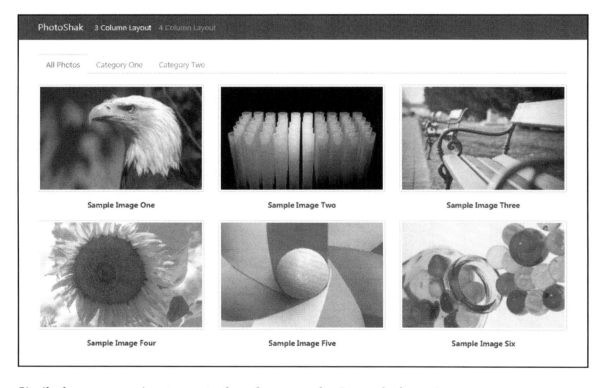

Similarly, we are going to create the other two tabs. Instead of creating two rows now, we will have only one row and we are going to add the first three images in **Category One** and the remaining three images in **Category Two**.

Here is the code for that:

```html
<div role="tabpanel" class="tab-pane" id="one">
    <div class="row">
      <div class="col-md-4">
        <a href="images/sample1.jpg" data-lightbox="gallery"
        data-title="Sample Image One">
          <img src="images/sample1.jpg" class="img-thumbnail">
        </a>
        <div class="title">Sample Image One</div>
      </div>
      <div class="col-md-4">
        <a href="images/sample2.jpg" data-lightbox="gallery"
        data-title="Sample Image Two">
          <img src="images/sample2.jpg" class="img-thumbnail">
        </a>
        <div class="title">Sample Image Two</div>
      </div>
      <div class="col-md-4">
        <a href="images/sample3.jpg" data-lightbox="gallery"
        data-title="Sample Image Three">
          <img src="images/sample3.jpg" class="img-thumbnail">
        </a>
        <div class="title">Sample Image Three</div>
      </div>
    </div>
</div>
<div role="tabpanel" class="tab-pane" id="two">
    <div class="row">
      <div class="col-md-4">
        <a href="images/sample4.jpg" data-lightbox="gallery"
        data-title="Sample Image Four">
          <img src="images/sample4.jpg" class="img-thumbnail">
        </a>
        <div class="title">Sample Image Four</div>
      </div>
      <div class="col-md-4">
        <a href="images/sample5.jpg" data-lightbox="gallery"
        data-title="Sample Image Five">
          <img src="images/sample5.jpg" class="img-thumbnail">
        </a>
        <div class="title">Sample Image Five</div>
      </div>
      <div class="col-md-4">
        <a href="images/sample6.jpg" data-lightbox="gallery"
        data-title="Sample Image Six">
          <img src="images/sample6.jpg" class="img-thumbnail">
        </a>
```

```
                 <div class="title">Sample Image Six</div>
              </div>
           </div>
        </div>
```

There you go. Now our tabs section is ready. There is no major difference in the code when compared to our **All Photos** code, we only have to rename a few things.

We are almost done building our website. The only thing that remains is the Sass code, so let's have a look at it:

```
body {
    padding-top:3.5rem;
}

section {
    margin:1.4 rem 0;
    padding:2rem 0;
}

.title {
    text-align:center;
    margin-top:1rem;
    margin-bottom: 1.4rem;
    font-weight:bold;
}

.carousel-item {
    img{width:100%;}
}
```

There is nothing much to explain here. Our website is ready now, so you can save the file and check it out.

We are done with the **3 Column Layout** now, so for our **4 Column Layout**, I will leave that for you to implement as an exercise. There is not going to be any major difference in the code except for the change in layout. You will have to create a new HTML page for that, maybe index2.html and instead of having three col-md-4, which put three images in one row, you will have to do four col-md-3 to get the **4 Column Layout**. You can always download the working code that comes with this book if you get stuck somewhere.

Alright, so with that, we are done with this website as well.

Summary

In this chapter, we saw how to create a `carousel` which had previous and next buttons. We also added bars in the `carousel`, which are basically the `carousel` indicators. Then, we created multiple tabs and populated them with images. After that, we saw how lightbox works. Finally, we learned how to create a **3 Column Layout**.

Other Books You May Enjoy

If you enjoyed this book, you may be interested in these other books by Packt:

Mastering Bootstrap 4 - Second Edition
Benjamin Jakobus

ISBN: 9781788834902

- Create a professional Bootstrap-based website from scratch without using third-party templates
- Leverage Bootstrap's powerful grid system
- Style various types of content and learn how to build a page's layout from scratch by applying the power of Bootstrap 4
- Take advantage of Bootstrap's form helper and contextual classes
- Improve your website's overall user experience with headers and footers
- Infuse your web pages using Bootstrap jQuery plugins and create your own Bootstrap plugins
- Learn what utility classes Bootstrap 4 has to offer, how they are implemented, and the best way to use them.
- Create more advanced web interfaces by leveraging the power of accordions, dropdowns, and list groups.
- Incorporate Bootstrap into an AngularJS or React application and use Bootstrap components as AngularJS directives

Vue.js 2 and Bootstrap 4 Web Development
Olga Filipova

ISBN: 9781788290920

- Create and build web applications using Vue.js, Webpack, and Nuxt.js
- Combine Bootstrap components with Vue.js' power to enrich your web applications with reusable elements
- Connect the Vuex state management architecture to the Firebase cloud backend to persist and manage application data
- Explore the new grid system of Bootstrap 4 along with the far simpler directives in Vue.js
- Test Vue applications using Jest
- Authenticate your application using Bootstrap's forms, Vue.js' reactivity, and Firebase's authentication API
- Deploy your application using Firebase, which provides Backend as a Service

Leave a review - let other readers know what you think

Please share your thoughts on this book with others by leaving a review on the site that you bought it from. If you purchased the book from Amazon, please leave us an honest review on this book's Amazon page. This is vital so that other potential readers can see and use your unbiased opinion to make purchasing decisions, we can understand what our customers think about our products, and our authors can see your feedback on the title that they have worked with Packt to create. It will only take a few minutes of your time, but is valuable to other potential customers, our authors, and Packt. Thank you!

Index

Printed in Great
Britain
by Amazon